15 MINUTE
SPANISH
LEARN IN JUST 12 WEEKS

ANA BREMÓN

DK
Penguin
Random
House

Senior Editors Angeles Gavira, Christine Stroyan
Project Art Editor Vanessa Marr
Jacket Design Development Manager Sophia MTT
Jacket Designer Juhi Sheth
Pre-Producer David Almond
Senior Producer Ana Vallarino
Associate Publisher Liz Wheeler
Publishing Director Jonathan Metcalf

**Language content for Dorling Kindersley by
g-and-w publishing.
Produced for Dorling Kindersley by
Schermuly Design Co.**

First American Edition, 2005
This revised edition published in the United States in 2018
by DK Publishing, 1450 Broadway, Suite 801,
New York, NY 10018, USA

18 19 20 21 22   10 9 8 7 6 5 4 3 2
003–187954–Jan/2018

CONTENTS

How to use this book   4

WEEK 1
INTRODUCTIONS
Hello   8
Relatives   10
My family   12
To be and to have   14
Review and repeat   16

WEEK 2
EATING AND DRINKING
In the café   18
In the restaurant   20
To want   22
Dishes   24
Review and repeat   26

WEEK 3
MAKING ARRANGEMENTS
Days and months   28
Time and numbers   30
Appointments   32
On the telephone   34
Review and repeat   36

WEEK 4
TRAVEL
At the ticket office   38
To go and to take   40
Taxi, bus, and metro   42
On the road   44
Review and repeat   46

WEEK 5
GETTING ABOUT
Around town 48
Directions 50
Sightseeing 52
At the airport 54
Review and repeat 56

WEEK 6
ACCOMMODATION
Booking a room 58
In the hotel 60
At the campground 62
Descriptions 64
Review and repeat 66

WEEK 7
SHOPPING
Shopping 68
At the market 70
At the supermarket 72
Clothes and shoes 74
Review and repeat 76

WEEK 8
WORK AND STUDY
Jobs 78
The office 80
Academic world 82
In business 84
Review and repeat 86

WEEK 9
HEALTH
At the pharmacy 88
The body 90
At the doctor 92
At the hospital 94
Review and repeat 96

WEEK 10
AT HOME
At home 98
Inside the house 100
The backyard 102
Pets 104
Review and repeat 106

WEEK 11
SERVICES
Bank and post office 108
Services 110
To come 112
Police and crime 114
Review and repeat 116

WEEK 12
LEISURE AND SOCIALIZING
Leisure time 118
Sport and hobbies 120
Socializing 122
Review and repeat 124
Reinforce and progress 126

MENU GUIDE 128

ENGLISH–SPANISH DICTIONARY ... 132

SPANISH–ENGLISH DICTIONARY ... 146

Acknowledgments 160

How to use this book

The main part of the book is devoted to 12 themed chapters, broken down into five 15-minute daily lessons, the last of which is a revision lesson. So, in just 12 weeks you will have completed the course. A concluding reference section contains a menu guide and English-to-Spanish and Spanish-to-English dictionaries.

Warm up
Each day starts with a warm up that encourages you to recall vocabulary or phrases you have learned previously. To the right of the heading bar you will see how long you need to spend on each exercise.

Instructions
Each exercise is numbered and introduced by instructions that explain what to do. In some cases additional information is given about the language point being covered.

Cultural/Conversational tip
These panels provide additional insights into life in Spain and language usage.

How to use the flap
The book's cover flaps allow you to conceal the Spanish so that you can test whether you have remembered correctly.

Revision pages
A recap of selected elements of previous lessons helps to reinforce your knowledge.

18   WEEK 2

1 Warm up (1 minute)

Count to ten. (pp.10-11)

Remind yourself how to say "hello" and "goodbye." (pp.8-9)

Ask "Do you have a son?" (pp.14-15)

EN LA CAFETERÍ
In the café

In a Spanish café you can get bread and p your coffee in the mornings. **Churros** (fri sticks) are a typical Spanish snack. You ca the counter or have waiter service at a tab to tip the waiter, but a few coins is usually

2 Words to remember (5 minutes)

Familiarize yourself with these words.

el té con limón *el tay kon leemon*	tea with lemon
el café descafeinado *el kafay deskafeynadoh*	decaffeinated coffee
el cortado *el kortadoh*	espresso with a bit of milk
la mermelada *lah mermeladah*	jam
la tostada con mantequilla *lah tostadah kon mantekee-yah*	toast with butter

el café solo
el kafay soloh
espresso

Cultural tip A standard coffee is small and black; if you want it any other way, you'll need to specify. If you want te with milk, ask for **té con leche**. If you just ask for **té**, you a likely to get tea with lemon.

3 In conversation (4 minutes)

Buenos días. Me pone un café con leche.
bwenos deeyas. may ponay oon kafay kon lechay

¿Eso es todo?
esoh es todoh

Is that all?

¿Tiene chur
tyenay choor

Do you have

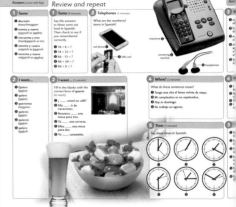

36   WEEK 2

Respuestas
Answers (Cover with flap)

REPASE Y REPITA
Review and repeat

MAKING ARRANG

Re
Ans

1 Sums
① **dieciséis** *deeyetheyseeyeys*
② **treinta y nueve** *trayntah ee nwebay*
③ **cincuenta y tres** *theenkwentah ee tres*
④ **setenta y cuatro** *setentah ee kwatroh*
⑤ **noventa y nueve** *nobentah ee nwebay*

1 Sums (4 minutes)
Say the answers to these sums out loud in Spanish. Then check to see if you remembered correctly.
① 10 + 6 = ?
② 14 + 25 = ?
③ 66 – 13 = ?
④ 40 + 34 = ?
⑤ 90 + 9 = ?

3 Telephones (3 minutes)
What are the numbered items in Spanish?

cell phone

SIM card

telephone

answering machine

headphones

3
①
②
③
④
⑤

2 I want...
① **Quiere** *kyairay*
② **quiere** *kyairay*
③ **queremos** *kerremos*
④ **quieres** *kyaires*
⑤ **quieren** *kyairen*
⑥ **quiero** *kyairoh*

2 I want... (3 minutes)
Fill in the blanks with the correct form of **querer** (to want).
① _____ usted un café?
② Ella _____ ir de vacaciones.
③ Nosotros _____ una mesa para tres.
④ Tú _____ una cerveza.
⑤ Ellos _____ una mesa para dos.
⑥ Yo _____ caramelos.

4 When? (2 minutes)
What do these sentences mean?
① Tengo una cita el lunes veinte de mayo.
② Mi cumpleaños es en septiembre.
③ Hoy es domingo.
④ No trabajo en agosto.

4
①
②
③
④

5 Time (3 minutes)
Say these times in Spanish.

5

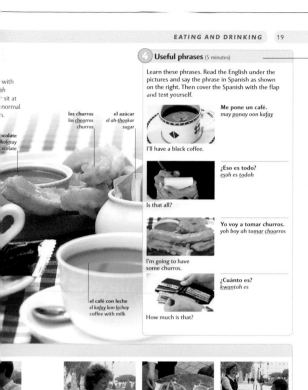

4 Useful phrases (5 minutes)

Learn these phrases. Read the English under the pictures and say the phrase in Spanish as shown on the right. Then cover the Spanish with the flap and test yourself.

with
sit at
normal

los churros
los choorros
churros

el azúcar
el ah-thookar
sugar

colate
kolatay
ocolate

el café con leche
el kafay kon lechay
coffee with milk

Me pone un café.
may ponay oon kafay

I'll have a black coffee.

¿Eso es todo?
esoh es todoh

Is that all?

Yo voy a tomar churros.
yoh boy ah tomar choorros

I'm going to have some churros.

¿Cuánto es?
kwantoh es

How much is that?

Useful phrases
Selected phrases relevant to the topic help you speak and understand.

Sí, señor.
see, senyor

Yes, sir.

Gracias. ¿Cuánto es?
grathyas. kwantoh es

Thank you. How much is that?

Cuatro euros, por favor.
kwatroh eh-ooros, por fabor

Four euros, please.

rros?

Text styles
Distinctive text styles differentiate Spanish and English, and the pronunciation guide.

In conversation
Illustrated dialogues reflecting how vocabulary and phrases are used in everyday situations appear throughout the book.

Say it
In these exercises you are asked to apply what you have learned using different vocabulary.

6 Say it (2 minutes)

Do you go near the train station?

Do you go near the Prado?

When is the next bus to Barcelona?

Dictionary
A mini-dictionary provides ready reference from English to Spanish and Spanish to English for 2,500 words.

Menu guide
Use this guide as a reference for food terminology and popular Spanish dishes.

Pronunciation guide

This book teaches European Spanish, which differs in pronunciation from the various dialects spoken in Latin America. A few Spanish sounds require special explanation:

c   a Spanish **c** is pronounced _th_ before **i** or **e** but **k** before other vowels: **cinco** <u>theen</u>koh (_five_)

h   **h** is always silent: **hola** o-lah (_hello_)

j (g)   a Spanish **j** (and **g** before **i** or **e**) is pronounced as a strong _h_, as if saying <u>hat</u> emphasizing the first letter

ll   pronounced _y_ as in _yes_

ñ   pronounced _ny_ like the sound in the middle of _canyon_

r   a Spanish **r** is trilled like a Scottish **r**, especially at the beginning of a word and when doubled

v   a Spanish **v** is halfway between an English _b_ and _v_

z   a Spanish **z** is pronounced _th_

Spanish vowels tend to be pronounced shorter than their English equivalents:

a   as the English _father_
e   as the English _wet_
i   as the English _keep_
o   as the English _boat_
u   as the English _boot_

After each word or phrase you will find a pronunciation transcription, with underlining showing the stress. Remember that this can only be an approximation; there is no substitute for listening to and mimicking native speakers.

How to use the audio app

All the numbered exercises in each lesson, apart from the Warm-ups at the beginning and the Say it exercises at the end, have recorded audio, available via a free app. The app also includes a function to record yourself and listen to yourself alongside native speakers.

To start using the audio with the book, first download the **DK 15 Minute Language Course** app on your smartphone or tablet from the App Store or Google Play. Open the app and scan the QR code on the back of this book to add it to your Library. As soon as the QR code is recognized, the audio will download.

There are two ways in which you can use the audio. The first is to read through your 15-minute lessons using the book only, and then go back and work with the audio and the book together, repeating the text in the gaps provided and then recording yourself. Or you can combine the book and the audio right from the beginning, pausing the app to read the instructions on the page as you need to. Try to say the words aloud, and practice enunciating properly. Detailed instructions on how to use the app are available from the menu bar in the app.

Remember that repetition is vital to language learning. The more often you listen to a conversation or repeat an oral exercise, the more the language will sink in.

Menu, Help/How to Use, Your Library

1 Getting started
The list of weeks will open when the audio has been downloaded. From here you can tap into each week's lessons.

When all the lessons in a week have been completed, the week button will be filled with color and show a check mark, so you can track your progress.

2 Lessons week by week
Each numbered exercise in a lesson is listed in the app as it appears in the book. Tap on an exercise to start.

A check mark indicates when an exercise has been completed.

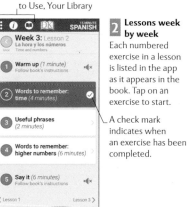

3 Audio for exercises
Tap the play button to hear instructions, then the exercise. You can pause the audio at any point, and return to it.

You can tap any part of the exercise to play the audio from that point.

4 Record yourself
When you are in the *Your recordings* screen, you can record yourself reading the words or participating in the conversations with native speakers, then listen back (and rerecord if desired).

Add recording
Play recording

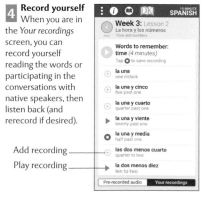

HOLA
Hello

1 **Warm up** (1 minute)

The Warm Up appears at the beginning of each lesson. It will remind you of what you have already learned and prepare you for moving ahead with the new subject.

In Spain, women often greet each other with one or two kisses on the cheek, and men shake other men's hands, although men may kiss or embrace younger male relatives or close friends. In formal situations—among strangers or in a business context—a handshake is the norm.

¡Hola!
o-lah
Hello!

2 **Words to remember** (2 minutes)

Look at these greetings and say them aloud. Conceal the text on the left with the cover flap and try to remember the Spanish for each item. Check your answers.

Buenos días. *bwenos deeyas*	Good morning/ day.
Me llamo Ana. *may yamoh anna*	My name is Ana.
Encantado/-a. *enkan-tadoh/-ah*	Pleased to meet you (man/woman speaking).
Buenas tardes (noches). *bwenas tardes (noches)*	Good afternoon/ evening (night).

Cultural tip The Spanish frequently address people as **señor** (*sir*), **señora** (*madam*, for older women), and **señorita** (*miss*, for young women). With first names use **Don** for men or **Doña** for women: **Don Juan**, **Doña Ana**.

3 **In conversation: formal** (3 minutes)

Buenos días. Me llamo Concha García.
bwenos deeyas. may yamoh konchah garthee-ah

Good day. My name's Concha García.

Señor López, encantado.
senyor lopeth, enkan-tadoh

Mr López, pleased to meet you.

Encantada.
enkan-tadah

Pleased to meet you.

4 Put into practice (3 minutes)

Join in this conversation. Read the Spanish beside the pictures on the left and then follow the instructions to make your reply. Then test yourself by concealing the answers on the right with the cover flap.

Buenas tardes señor. **Buenas tardes señora.**
bwenas tardes senyor _bwenas tardes senyorah_

Good evening, sir.

Say: Good evening, madam.

Me llamo Julia. **Encantado.**
may yamoh hoolya _enkan-tadoh_

My name is Julia.

Say: Pleased to meet you.

5 Useful phrases (3 minutes)

Read these phrases aloud several times and try to memorize them. Conceal the Spanish with the cover flap and test yourself.

What's your name?	**¿Cómo se llama?** _komo seh yamah_
Goodbye.	**Adiós.** _addy-os_
Thank you.	**Gracias.** _grathyas_
See you soon/tomorrow.	**Hasta pronto/mañana.** _astah prontoh/manyanah_

6 In conversation: informal (3 minutes)

Entonces, ¿hasta mañana?
entonthes, astah manyanah

So, see you tomorrow?

Sí, adiós.
see, addy-os

Yes, goodbye.

Adiós. Hasta pronto.
addy-os. astah prontoh

Goodbye. See you soon.

LAS RELACIONES
Relatives

The Spanish equivalents of *mom* and *dad* are **mamá** and **papá**. The male plural can refer to both sexes–for example, **niños** (*boys* and *children*), **padres** (*fathers* and *parents*), **abuelos** (*grandfathers* and *grandparents*), **tíos** (*uncles* and *aunt and uncle*), **hermanos** (*brothers* and *siblings*), and so on.

2 **Match and repeat** (5 minutes)

Look at the people in this scene and match their numbers with the list at the side. Read the Spanish words aloud. Then conceal the list with the cover flap and test yourself.

❶ **la hermana**
   lah airmanah

❷ **el abuelo**
   el abweloh

❸ **el padre**
   el pahdray

❹ **el hermano**
   el airmanoh

❺ **la abuela**
   lah abwelah

❻ **la hija**
   lah ee-hah

❼ **la madre**
   lah mahdray

❽ **el hijo**
   el ee-hoh

grandfather ❷   ❸ father

sister ❶   ❹ brother

❺ grandmother   ❻ daughter   ❼ mother   ❽ son

Conversational tip In Spanish, things as well as people are masculine or feminine–for example, *wine* is masculine (**el vino**) but *milk* is feminine (**la leche**). Use **los** and **las** for masculine and feminine plurals, respectively. For *a/an*, use **un** for masculine and **una** for feminine items.

3 Words to remember: relatives (4 minutes)

el marido
el mareedoh
husband

la mujer
lah moo-hair
wife

Estoy casado/-a.
estoy kasadoh/-ah
I'm married (m/f).

Familiarize yourself with these words. Read them aloud several times and try to memorize them. Conceal the Spanish with the cover flap and test yourself.

father/mother-in-law	**el suegro/la suegra** *el swegroh/lah swegrah*
stepfather	**el padrastro** *el padras-troh*
stepmother	**la madrastra** *lah madras-trah*
children (male/female)	**los niños/las niñas** *los neenyos/las neenyas*
uncle/aunt	**el tío/la tía** *el tee-oh/lah tee-ah*
cousin	**el primo/la prima** *el preemoh/lah preemah*
I have four children.	**Tengo cuatro niños.** *tengoh kwatroh neenyos*
I have two stepdaughters and a stepson.	**Tengo dos hijastras y un hijastro.** *tengoh dos ee-hastras ee oon ee-hastroh*

4 Words to remember: numbers (3 minutes)

Memorize these words and then test yourself using the cover flap.

Be careful when you use the number one. When you use **uno** in front of a word, it changes to **un** or **una**, depending on whether that word is masculine or feminine. For example: **Tengo un hijo** (*I have one son*), **Tengo una hija** (*I have one daughter*).

one	**uno/-a** *oonoh/-ah*
two	**dos** *dos*
three	**tres** *tres*
four	**cuatro** *kwatroh*
five	**cinco** *theenkoh*
six	**seis** *seys*
seven	**siete** *syetay*
eight	**ocho** *ochoh*
nine	**nueve** *nwebay*
ten	**diez** *dyeth*

5 Say it (2 minutes)

I have five sons.

I have three sisters and a brother.

I have two children.

1 Warm up (1 minute)

Say the Spanish for as many members of the family as you can. (pp.10-11)

Say "I have two sons." (pp.10-11)

MI FAMILIA
My family

There are two ways of saying *you* in Spanish, **usted** for formal situations and **tú** in informal ones. There is also a formal way of saying *your*—**su** (singular) and **sus** (plural): **usted y su mujer** (*you and your wife*), **¿Son ésos sus hijos?** (*Are those your sons?*). **Su** and **sus** also mean *his* and *her*.

2 Words to remember (5 minutes)

Say these words aloud a few times. Conceal the Spanish with the cover flap and try to remember the Spanish word for each item.

mi *mee*	my (with singular)
mis *mees*	my (with plural)
tu *too*	your (informal with singular)
tus *toos*	your (informal with plural)
su *soo*	your (formal with singular)
sus *soos*	your (formal with plural)
su *soo*	his/her (with singular) their (with singular)
sus *soos*	his/her (with plural) their (with plural)

Éstos son mis padres.
estos son mees pahdres
These are my parents.

3 In conversation (4 minutes)

¿Tiene usted niños?
tyenay oosted neenyos

Do you have any children?

Sí, tengo dos hijas.
see, tengoh dos ee-has

Yes, I have two daughters.

Éstas son mis hijas.
¿Y usted?
estas son mees ee-has.
ee oosted

These are my daughters. And you?

Conversational tip The Spanish ask a question by simply raising the pitch of the voice at the end of a statement: **¿Quieres un poco de vino?** (*Do you want a little wine?*). Notice the upside-down question mark (**¿**) written at the beginning of the question. You will also see an upside-down exclamation mark, as in **¡Hola!** (*Hello!*).

4 Useful phrases (3 minutes)

Read these phrases aloud several times and try to memorize them. Conceal the Spanish with the cover flap and test yourself.

Do you have any brothers? (formal)	**¿Tiene usted hermanos?** *tyenay oosted airmanos*
Do you have any brothers? (informal)	**¿Tienes hermanos?** *tyenes airmanos*

This is my husband.	**Éste es mi marido.** *estay es mee mareedoh*
That's my wife.	**Ésa es mi mujer.** *esah es mee moo-hair*

Is that your sister? (formal)	**¿Es ésa su hermana?** *es esah soo airmanah*
Is that your sister? (informal)	**¿Es ésa tu hermana?** *es esah too airmanah*

5 Say it (2 minutes)

Do you have any brothers and sisters? (formal)

Do you have any children? (informal)

I have two sisters.

This is my wife, María.

No, pero tengo un hijastro.
noh, peroh tengoh oon ee-hastroh

No, but I have a stepson.

1 Warm up (1 minute)

Say "See you soon."
(pp.8-9)

Say "I am married"
(pp.10-11) and "I have
a wife." (pp.12-13)

SER Y TENER
To be and to have

Two of the most important verbs are **ser** (*to be*)
and **tener** (*to have*). Note that there are different
ways of saying *you*, *we*, and *they*, with formal and
informal, singular and plural, and masculine
and feminine forms. Pronouns (*I*, *you*, etc.) are
omitted where the sense is clear.

2 Ser: to be (5 minutes)

Familiarize yourself with **ser** (*to be*). When you are
confident, practice the sample sentences below.
Note: there is another verb meaning "to be"–**estar**,
which is discussed on page 49.

yo soy *yoh soy*	I am
tú eres *too eh-res*	you are (informal singular)
usted es *oosted es*	you are (formal singular)
él/ella es *el/eh-yah es*	he/she is
nosotros/-as somos *nosotros/-as somos*	we are (masculine/feminine)
vosotros/-as sois *bosotros/-as soys*	you are (informal plural, m/f)
ustedes son *oostedes son*	you are (formal plural)
ellos/-as son *eh-yos/-yas son*	they are (masculine/feminine)

Yo soy inglesa.
yoh soy eenglesah
I'm English.

¿De dónde es usted? *day donday es oosted*	Where are you from?
Es mi hermana. *es mee airmanah*	She is my sister.
Somos españoles. *somos espanyoles*	We're Spanish.

3 Tener: to have (5 minutes)

Practice **tener** (*to have*) and the sample sentences, then test yourself.

I have	**yo tengo** *yoh tengoh*
you have (informal singular)	**tú tienes** *too tyenes*
you have (formal singular)	**usted tiene** *oosted tyenay*
he/she has	**él/ella tiene** *el/eh-yah tyenay*
we have (masculine/feminine)	**nosotros/-as tenemos** *nosotros/-as tenaymos*
you have (informal plural, m/f)	**vosotros/-as teneis** *bosotros/-as tenays*
you have (formal plural)	**ustedes tienen** *oostedes tyenen*
they have (masculine/feminine)	**ellos/-as tienen** *eh-yos/-yas tyenen*

¿Tiene rosas rojas?
tyenay rosas rohas
Do you have red roses?

He has a meeting.	**Tiene una reunión.** *tyenay oonah re-oonyon*
Do you have a cell phone?	**¿Tiene usted móvil?** *tyenay oosted mobeel?*
How many brothers and sisters do you have?	**¿Cuántos hermanos tiene usted?** *kwantos airmanos tyenay oosted*

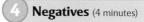

4 Negatives (4 minutes)

la bicicleta
lah beetheekletah
bicycle

It is easy to make sentences negative in Spanish; just put **no** in front of the verb:
No somos americanos (*We're not American*).

I'm not Spanish.	**No soy español.** *noh soy espanyol*
He's not a vegetarian.	**No es vegetariano.** *noh es be-hetaryanoh*
We don't have any children.	**No tenemos niños.** *noh tenaymos neenyos*

No tengo coche.
noh tengoh kochay
I don't have a car.

Respuestas
Answers (Cover with flap)

REPASE Y REPITA
Review and repeat

1 How many

❶ **tres**
tres

❷ **nueve**
nwebay

❸ **cuatro**
kwatroh

❹ **dos**
dos

❺ **ocho**
ochoh

❻ **diez**
dyeth

❼ **cinco**
theenkoh

❽ **siete**
syetay

❾ **seis**
seys

1 How many (2 minutes)

Cover the answers with the cover flap. Then say these Spanish numbers out loud. Check to see if you remembered the Spanish correctly.

3 ❶
9 ❷
4 ❸
2 ❹
8 ❺
10 ❻
5 ❼
7 ❽
6 ❾

2 Hello

❶ **Buenos días. Me llamo... [your name].**
bwenos deeyas. may yamoh...

❷ **Encantado/-a.**
enkan-tadoh/-ah

❸ **Sí, y tengo dos hijos. ¿Y usted?**
see, ee tengoh dos ee-hos. ee oosted

❹ **Adiós. Hasta mañana.**
addy-os. astah manyanah

2 Hello (4 minutes)

You are talking to someone you have just met. Join in the conversation, replying in Spanish following the English prompts.

Buenos días. Me llamo María.
❶ Answer the greeting and give your name.

Éste es mi marido, Juan.
❷ Say "Pleased to meet you."

¿Está usted casado/-a?
❸ Say "Yes, and I have two sons. And you?"

Nosotros tenemos tres hijos.
❹ Say "Goodbye. See you tomorrow."

3 To have or be (5 minutes)

Fill in the blanks with the correct form of **tener** (*to have*) or **ser** (*to be*). Check to see if you have remembered the Spanish correctly.

❶ Yo ___ americana.

❷ Nosotros ___ cuatro niños.

❸ Yo no ___ feliz.

❹ ¿ ___ tú coche?

❺ Él ___ mi marido.

❻ Yo no ___ teléfono móvil.

❼ Tú no ___ español.

❽ ¿ ___ usted hijos?

3 To have or be

❶ **soy**
soy

❷ **tenemos**
tenaymos

❸ **soy**
soy

❹ **tienes**
tyenes

❺ **es**
es

❻ **tengo**
tengoh

❼ **eres**
eh-res

❽ **tiene**
tyenay

4 Family (4 minutes)

Say the Spanish for each of the numbered family members. Check to see if you have remembered the Spanish correctly.

grandfather ❷   ❸ father
sister ❶   ❹ brother
❺ grandmother   ❻ daughter   ❼ mother   ❽ son

4 Family

❶ **la hermana**
lah airmanah

❷ **el abuelo**
el abweloh

❸ **el padre**
el pahdray

❹ **el hermano**
el airmanoh

❺ **la abuela**
lah abwelah

❻ **la hija**
lah ee-hah

❼ **la madre**
lah mahdray

❽ **el hijo**
el ee-hoh

Warm up (1 minute)

Count to ten. (pp.10-11)

Remind yourself how to say "hello" and "goodbye." (pp.8-9)

Ask "Do you have a son?" (pp.14-15)

EN LA CAFETERÍA
In the café

In a Spanish café you can get bread and pastries with your coffee in the mornings. **Churros** (*fried dough sticks*) are a typical Spanish snack. You can either sit at the counter or have waiter service at a table. It is normal to tip the waiter, but a few coins is usually enough.

el chocolate
el chokolatay
hot chocolate

2   **Words to remember** (5 minutes)

Familiarize yourself with these words.

el té con limón *el tay kon leemon*	tea with lemon
el café descafeinado *el kafay deskafeynadoh*	decaffeinated coffee
el cortado *el kortadoh*	espresso with a bit of milk
la mermelada *lah mermeladah*	jam
la tostada con mantequilla *lah tostadah kon mantekee-yah*	toast with butter

el café solo
el kafay soloh
espresso

Cultural tip A standard coffee is small and black; if you want it any other way, you'll need to specify. If you want tea with milk, ask for **té con leche**. If you just ask for **té**, you are likely to get tea with lemon.

3   **In conversation** (4 minutes)

Buenos días. Me pone un café con leche.
bwenos deeyas. may ponay oon kafay kon lechay

Hello. I'll have coffee with milk, please.

¿Eso es todo?
esoh es todoh

Is that all?

¿Tiene churros?
tyenay choorros

Do you have any churros?

4 Useful phrases (5 minutes)

Learn these phrases. Read the English under the pictures and say the phrase in Spanish as shown on the right. Then cover the Spanish with the flap and test yourself.

los churros
los _choorros_
churros

el azúcar
el ah-_thookar_
sugar

el café con leche
el _kafay_ kon _lechay_
coffee with milk

Me pone un café.
may ponay oon kafay

I'll have a black coffee.

¿Eso es todo?
esoh es todoh

Is that all?

Yo voy a tomar churros.
yoh boy ah tomar choorros

I'm going to have some churros.

¿Cuánto es?
kwantoh es

How much is that?

Sí, señor.
see, senyor

Yes, sir.

Gracias. ¿Cuánto es?
grathyas. kwantoh es

Thank you. How much is that?

Cuatro euros, por favor.
kwatroh eh-ooros, por fabor

Four euros, please.

EN EL RESTAURANTE
In the restaurant

1 **Warm up** (1 minute)

Ask "How much is that?"
(pp.18-19)

Say "I don't have a
brother." (pp.14-15)

Ask "Do you have any
churros?" (pp.18-19)

There are a variety of different types of eating places
in Spain. In a bar or **tasca** you can find a few **tapas** or
snacks. Lunch is the main meal of the day, but if you
are not very hungry, many restaurants offer **tapas** at
the bar, which is usually very economica or a light meal.

2 **Words to remember** (3 minutes)

Memorize these words. Conceal
the Spanish with the cover flap
and test yourself.

la carta *lah <u>kar</u>tah*	menu
la carta de vinos *lah <u>kar</u>tah day <u>bee</u>nos*	wine list
los entrantes *los en<u>tran</u>tes*	appetizers
el plato principal *el <u>pla</u>toh preen<u>thee</u><u>pal</u>*	main course
los postres *los <u>pos</u>tres*	desserts
el desayuno *el desah-<u>yoo</u>noh*	breakfast
el almuerzo *el almoo<u>air</u>thoh*	lunch
la cena *lah <u>the</u>nah*	dinner

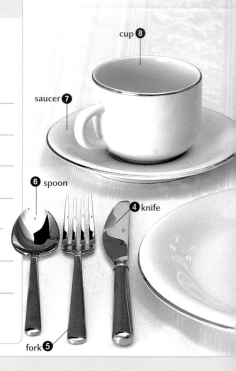

cup **8**

saucer **7**

6 spoon

4 knife

fork **5**

3 **In conversation** (4 minutes)

**Hola. Una mesa para
cuatro, por favor.**
*o-lah. <u>oo</u>nah <u>me</u>sah <u>pa</u>rah
<u>kwa</u>troh, por fa<u>bor</u>*

Hello. A table for
four, please.

¿Tiene una reserva?
<u>tye</u>nay <u>oo</u>nah re<u>ser</u>bah

Do you have a reservation?

Sí, a nombre de Cortés.
see, ah <u>nom</u>bray day kor<u>tes</u>

Yes, in the name of Cortés.

4 Match and repeat (4 minutes)

Look at the numbered objects on this table and match them with
the items in the vocabulary list at the side. Read the Spanish words
aloud. Now, conceal the list with the cover flap and test yourself.

glass ❶

❷ napkin

plate ❸

❶ la copa
  lah kopah

❷ la servilleta
  lah serbee-yetah

❸ el plato
  el platoh

❹ el cuchillo
  el koochee-yoh

❺ el tenedor
  el tenedor

❻ la cuchara
  lah koocharah

❼ el platillo
  el plateeyoh

❽ la taza
  lah tathah

5 Useful phrases (4 minutes)

Learn these phrases and then test yourself using the
cover flap to conceal the Spanish.

What do you have for dessert?	**¿Qué tiene de postre?** *kay tyenay day postray*
The check, please.	**La cuenta, por favor.** *lah kwentah, por fabor*

**Muy bien. ¿Qué mesa
le gustaría?**
*mwee byen. kay mesah
le goostareeyah*

Very good. Which table
would you like?

**Cerca de la ventana,
por favor.**
*therkah day lah bentanah,
por fabor*

Near the
window please.

Síganme, por favor.
seegan-may, por fabor.

Follow me, please.

Warm up (1 minute)

What are "breakfast," "lunch," and "dinner" in Spanish? (pp.20-1)

Say "I," "you" (informal), "he," "she," "we," "you" (plural/formal), "they" (masculine), "they" (feminine). (pp.14-15)

QUERER
To want

Querer (*to want*) is a verb that is essential to everyday conversation. There is also a polite form, **quisiera** (*I'd like*). Use this when requesting something because **quiero** (*I want*) may sound too strong: **¿Qué quiere beber?** (*What do you want to drink?*); **Quisiera una cerveza** (*I'd like a beer*).

Querer: to want (6 minutes)

Say the different forms of **querer** (*to want*) aloud. Use the cover flap to test yourself and, when you are confident, practice the sample sentences below.

yo quiero *yoh kyairoh*	I want
tú quieres/usted quiere *too kyaires/oosted kyairay*	you want (singular, informal/formal)
él/ella quiere *el/eh-yah kyairay*	he/she wants
nosotros/-as queremos *nosotros/-as keraymos*	we want (masculine/feminine)
vosotros/-as queréis **ustedes quieren** *bosotros/-as kerays/oostedes kyairen*	you want (plural, informal/formal)
ellos/-as quieren *eh-yos/-as-yas kyairen*	they want (masculine/feminine)
¿Quieres vino? *kyaires beenoh?*	Do you want some wine?
Quiere un coche nuevo. *kyairay oon kochay nweboh*	She wants a new car.

Quiero caramelos.
kyairoh karamelos
I want some candy.

Conversational tip Although it may sound rude to you, Spaniards don't say *please* (**por favor**) or *thank you* (**gracias**) very often, and they hardly ever say *excuse me* (**perdón**) or *I'm sorry* (**lo siento**), but they use the tone of their voices and choice of words to imply politeness, such as **quisiera** (*I'd like*) instead of **quiero** (*I want*).

3 Polite requests (4 minutes)

Practice the following sample phrases that use **quisiera** (*I'd like*), the form of **quiero** (*I want*) that is used for polite requests.

I'd like a beer.	**Quisiera un cerveza.** *keesyairah oon therbaythah*
I'd like a table for tonight.	**Quisiera una mesa para esta noche.** *keesyairah oonah mesah parah estah nocheh*
I'd like to see the menu, please.	**Quisiera ver la carta, por favor.** *keesyairah ber lah kartah, por fabor*

4 Put into practice (4 minutes)

Join in this conversation. Read the Spanish beside the pictures on the left and follow the instructions to make your reply. Then test yourself by concealing the answers using the cover flap.

Buenas tardes señor. ¿Tiene una reserva?
bwenas tardes senyor. tyeneh oonah reserbah

Good evening, sir. Do you have a reservation?

Say: No, but I would like a table for three.

No, pero quisiera una mesa para tres.
noh, peroh keesyairah oonah mesah parah tres

Muy bien. ¿Qué mesa le gustaría?
mwee byen. kay mesah le goostareeyah

Fine. Which table would you like?

Say: Near the window, please.

Cerca de la ventana, por favor.
therkah day lah bentanah, por fabor

LOS PLATOS
Dishes

Spain offers a large variety of regional dishes. Plenty of garlic and olive oil are a feature of many typical recipes. Restaurants do not normally offer a vegetarian menu; there are, however, many traditional Spanish dishes that do not contain any meat. Ask your waiter for advice.

1 Warm up (1 minute)

Say "I'm Spanish" and "She has a bicycle." (pp.14-15)

Ask "Do you have churros?" (pp.18-19)

Say "I'd like coffee with milk." (pp.18-19)

Cultural tip At lunch time, you will find many restaurants offer **el menú del día** (*the day's set menu*). This is usually a three-course meal with bread and a drink included in the price.

2 Match and repeat (4 minutes)

Match the numbered items to the Spanish words in the panel.

1 las verduras
las berdooras

2 la fruta
lah frootah

3 el queso
el kesoh

4 los frutos secos
los frootos sekos

5 la sopa
lah sopah

6 las aves
las ahbes

7 el pescado
el peskadoh

8 la pasta
lah pastah

9 el marisco
el mareeskoh

10 la carne
lah karnay

fruit **2**

vegetables **1**

cheese **3**

5 soup

poultry **6**

8 pasta

9 seafood

3 Words to remember: cooking methods (3 minutes)

The ending often varies depending on the gender of item described.

fried (m/f)	**frito/-a**	_free_toh/-ah
grilled	**a la plancha**	ah lah _plan_chah
roasted (m/f)	**asado/-a**	ah_sa_doh/-ah
boiled (m/f)	**hervido/-a**	er_bee_doh/-ah
steamed	**al vapor**	al ba_por_
rare (m/f)	**poco hecho/-a**	pokoh _eh_-choh/-ah

Quisiera mi filete bien hecho.
kees_yai_rah mee _fee_letay byen _eh_-choh
I'd like my steak well done.

6 Say it (2 minutes)

What is **tortilla**?

I'm allergic to seafood.

I'd like a beer.

4 Words to remember: drinks (3 minutes)

Familiarize yourself with these words.

water	**el agua**	el _ah_gwah
sparkling water	**el agua con gas**	el _ah_gwah kon gas
still water	**el agua sin gas**	el _ah_gwah seen gas
wine	**el vino**	el _bee_noh
beer	**la cerveza**	lah thair_bay_thah
fruit juice	**el zumo**	el _thoo_moh

nuts

fish 7

10 meat

5 Useful phrases (2 minutes)

Learn these phrases and then test yourself.

I am a vegetarian. (m/f).	**Soy vegetariano/-a.** soy be-heta_reea_noh/-ah
I am allergic to nuts. (m/f)	**Soy alérgico/-a a los frutos secos.** soy ah_ler_-heekoh/-ah ah los _froo_tos _se_kos
What is "conejo"?	**¿Qué es "conejo"?** kay es ko_ne_-hoh

Respuestas
Answers (Cover with flap)

REPASE Y REPITA
Review and repeat

1 What food?

❶ **los frutos secos**
los frootos sekos

❷ **el marisco**
el mareeskoh

❸ **la carne**
lah karnay

❹ **el azúcar**
el ah-thookar

❺ **la copa**
lah kopah

1 What food? (4 minutes)

Name the numbered items.

❶ nuts

sugar ❹

seafood ❷

meat ❸

glass ❺

2 This is my...

❶ **Ésta es mi mujer.**
estah es mee moo-hair

❷ **Aquí están sus hijas.**
*ahkee estan soos
ee-has*

❸ **Su mesa es de no
fumadores.**
*soo mesah es day noh
foomadores*

2 This is my... (4 minutes)

Say these phrases in Spanish. Use **mi(-s)**, **tu(-us)**
or **su(-s)**.

❶ This is my wife.
❷ Here are her
daughters.
❸ Their table is
non-smoking.

3 I'd like...

❶ **Quisiera un café.**
keesyairah oon kafay

❷ **Quisiera churros.**
keesyairah choorros

❸ **Quisiera azúcar.**
keesyairah ah-thookar

❹ **Quisiera un café
con leche.**
*keesyairah oon kafay
kon lechay*

3 I'd like... (3 minutes)

Say "I'd like" the following:

❶ black coffee   churros ❷   ❸ sugar

coffee with milk ❹

Respuestas
Answers (Cover with flap)

1 What food?

6 la pasta
lah pastah

7 el cuchillo
el koochee yoh

8 el queso
el kesoh

9 la servilleta
lah serbee-yetah

10 la cerveza
lah thairbaythah

6 pasta
knife **7**
8 cheese
beer **10**
9 napkin

4 Restaurant (4 minutes)

You arrive at a restaurant. Join in the conversation, replying in Spanish following the English prompts.

Buenas tardes señora, señor.
1 Ask for a table for six.

¿Fumadores o no fumadores?
2 Say: nonsmoking.

Síganme, por favor.
3 Ask for the menu.

¿Quiere la carta de vinos?
4 Say: No. Sparkling water, please.

Muy bien.
5 Say you don't have a glass.

4 Restaurant

1 Buenas tardes, quisiera una mesa para seis.
bwenas tardes, keesyairah oonah mesah parah seys

2 No fumadores.
noh foomadores

3 La carta, por favor.
lah kartah, por fabor

4 No. Agua con gas, por favor.
noh. ahgwah kon gas, por fabor

5 No tengo copa.
noh tengoh kopah

LOS DÍAS Y LOS MESES
Days and months

1 Warm up (1 minute)

Say "he is" and "they are." (pp.14-15)

Say "he is not" and "they are not." (pp.14-15)

What is Spanish for "the children"? (pp.10-11)

In Spanish, *days of the week* (**los días de la semana**) and *months* (**los meses**) do not have capital letters. Note that you use **en** with months: **en abril** (*in April*), but **el** or **los** with days: **el/los lunes** (*on Monday/Mondays*).

2 Words to remember: days of the week (5 minutes)

Familiarize yourself with these words and test yourself using the cover flap.

lunes *loones*	Monday
martes *martes*	Tuesday
miércoles *myairkoles*	Wednesday
jueves *hwebes*	Thursday
viernes *byernes*	Friday
sábado *sabadoh*	Saturday
domingo *domeengoh*	Sunday
hoy *oy*	today
mañana *manyanah*	tomorrow
ayer *ah-yair*	yesterday

Nos reunimos mañana.
mos reh-ooneemos manyanah
We meet tomorrow.

Tengo una reserva para hoy.
tengoh oonah reserbah parah oy
I have a reservation for today.

3 Useful phrases: days (2 minutes)

Learn these phrases and then test yourself using the cover flap.

La reunión no es el martes. *lah reh-oonyon noh es el martes*	The meeting isn't on Tuesday.
Trabajo los domingos. *traba-hoh los domeengos*	I work on Sundays.

4 Words to remember: months (5 minutes)

Familiarize yourself with these words and test yourself using the cover flap.

Nuestro aniversario es en julio.
nwestroh aneebairsaree-oh es en hoolee-oh
Our anniversary is in July.

Navidad es en diciembre.
nabeedad es en deethyembray
Christmas is in December.

January	**enero**	*ehneroh*
February	**febrero**	*febreroh*
March	**marzo**	*marthoh*
April	**abril**	*abreel*
May	**mayo**	*mah-yoh*
June	**junio**	*hoonee-oh*
July	**julio**	*hoolee-oh*
August	**agosto**	*agostoh*
September	**septiembre**	*septyembray*
October	**octubre**	*oktoobray*
November	**noviembre**	*nobyembray*
December	**diciembre**	*deethyembray*
month	**el mes**	*el mes*
year	**el año**	*el anyoh*

5 Useful phrases: months (2 minutes)

Learn these phrases and then test yourself using the cover flap.

My children are on vacation in August.
Mis hijos están de vacaciones en agosto.
mees ee-hos estan day bakathyones en agostoh

My birthday is in June.
Mi cumpleaños es en junio.
mee koomplay-anyos es en hoonee-oh

1 **Warm up** (1 minute)

Count in Spanish from 1 to 10. (pp.10-11)

Say "I have a reservation." (pp.20-1)

Say "The meeting is on Wednesday." (pp.28-9)

LA HORA Y LOS NÚMEROS
Time and numbers

The hour is preceded by **la** as in **la una** (*one o'clock*) and **las** for other numbers: **las dos**, **las tres**, and so on. In English the minutes sometimes come first (*ten to five*); in Spanish the hour comes first: **las cinco menos diez** (*five minus ten*).

2 **Words to remember: time** (4 minutes)

Memorize how to tell the time in Spanish.

la una *lah oonah*	one o'clock
la una y cinco *lah oonah ee theenkoh*	five after one
la una y cuarto *lah oonah ee kwartoh*	one-fifteen
la una y veinte *lah oonah ee beyntay*	one-twenty
la una y media *lah oonah ee medee-ah*	one-thirty
las dos menos cuarto *las dos menos kwartoh*	quarter to two
las dos menos diez *las dos menos dyeth*	ten to two

3 **Useful phrases** (2 minutes)

Learn these phrases and then test yourself using the cover flap.

¿Qué hora es? *kay orah es*	What time is it?
¿A qué hora quiere el desayuno? *ah kay orah kyairay el desah-yoonoh*	What time do you want breakfast?
La reunión es a mediodía. *lah reh-oonyon es ah maydyodee-ah*	The meeting is at noon.

4 Words to remember: higher numbers (6 minutes)

To say 21 you use **veinti** and add **uno** (*one*): **veintiuno**. Successive numbers are created in the same way—for example, **veintidós** (22), **veintitrés** (23), and so on. After 30, link the numbers with **y** (*and*): **treinta y uno** (31), **cuarenta y cinco** (45), **sesenta y seis** (66).

Note the special forms used for 500, 700, and 900: **quinientos**, **setecientos**, and **novecientos**.

Quiero el autobús cincuenta y tres.
kyairoh el aootoboos theenkwentah ee tres
I want the route 53 bus.

eleven	**once**	*onthay*
twelve	**doce**	*dothay*
thirteen	**trece**	*trethay*
fourteen	**catorce**	*katorthay*
fifteen	**quince**	*keenthay*
sixteen	**dieciséis**	*deeaytheeseyees*
seventeen	**diecisiete**	*deeaytheesyeytay*
eighteen	**dieciocho**	*deeaythyochoh*
nineteen	**diecinueve**	*deeaythynwebay*
twenty	**veinte**	*beyntay*
thirty	**treinta**	*treyntah*
forty	**cuarenta**	*kwarentah*
fifty	**cincuenta**	*theenkwentah*
sixty	**sesenta**	*sesentah*
seventy	**setenta**	*setentah*
eighty	**ochenta**	*ochentah*
ninety	**noventa**	*nobentah*
one hundred	**cien**	*theeayn*
two hundred	**doscientos**	*dos-theeayntos*
five hundred	**quinientos**	*keeneeayntos*
one thousand	**mil**	*meel*
two thousand	**dos mil**	*dos meel*
one million	**un millón**	*oon mee-yon*

5 Say it (2 minutes)

25

68

84

91

five to ten

eleven-thirty

What time is lunch?

1 Warm up (1 minute)

Say the days of the week.
(pp.28-9)

Say "three o'clock."
(pp.30-1)

What's the Spanish for
"today," "tomorrow," and
"yesterday"? (pp.28-9)

LAS CITAS
Appointments

Business in Spain is generally conducted more
formally than in the United States. The Spanish
also tend to leave the office for the lunch hour,
often having a sit-down meal. Remember to use
the formal forms of *you* (**usted, ustedes**) in
business situations.

Bienvenido.
byenveneedoh
Welcome.

2 Useful phrases (5 minutes)

Learn these phrases and then test yourself.

¿Nos reunimos mañana? *nos reh-ooneemos* *manyanah*	Shall we meet tomorrow?
¿Con quién? *kon kee-en*	With whom?
¿Cuándo está libre? *kwandoh esta leebray*	When are you free?
Lo siento, estoy **ocupado(-a).** *loh syentoh, estoy* *okoopadoh(-ah)*	I'm sorry, I'm busy.
¿Qué tal el jueves? *keh tal el hwebes*	How about Thursday?
A mí me va bien. *ah mee may bah byen*	That's good for me.

el apretón
de manos
el apreton
day manos
handshake

3 In conversation (4 minutes)

**Buenos días. Tengo
una cita.**
*bwenos deeyas. tengoh
oonah theetah*

Good morning. I have
an appointment.

¿Con quién es la cita?
kon kee-en es lah theetah

With whom is
the appointment?

Con el Señor Montoya.
kon el senyor montoyah

With Mr. Montoya.

4 Put into practice (5 minutes)

Join in this conversation. Read the Spanish beside the pictures on the left and then follow the instructions to make your reply. Then test yourself by concealing the answers on the right with the cover flap.

¿Nos reunimos el jueves?
nos reh-ooneemos el hwebes?

Shall we meet Thursday?

Say: Sorry, I'm busy

Lo siento, estoy ocupado(-a).
loh syentoh, estoy okoopadoh(-ah)

¿Cuándo está libre?
kwandoh esta leebray

When are you free?

Say: Tuesday afternoon.

El martes por la tarde.
el martes por lah tarday

A mí me va bien.
ah mee may bah byen

That's good for me.

Ask: At what time?

¿A qué hora?
ah kay orah

A las cuatro, si a usted le va bien.
ah las kwatroh, see ah oosted le bah byen

At four o'clock, if that's good for you.

Say: Yes, it's good for me.

Sí, me va bien.
see, may bah byen

Muy bien. ¿A qué hora?
mwee byen. ah kay orah?

Okay. What time?

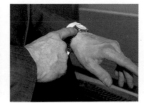

A las tres, pero llego un poco tarde.
ah las tres, peroh yegoh oon pokoh tarday

At three o'clock, but I'm a little late.

No se preocupe. Tome asiento, por favor.
noh say pre-ohkoopay. tomay asyaintoh, por fabor

Don't worry. Take a seat, please.

POR TELÉFONO
On the telephone

1 Warm up (1 minute)

Say "I'm sorry." (pp.32-3)

What is the Spanish for "I'd like an appointment"? (pp.32-3)

How do you say "when?" in Spanish? (pp.32-3)

The emergency number for police, ambulance, or fire services is 112. For directory assistance, dial 11818. If you are planning to make a lot of phone calls from Spain, the most cost-effective option is to buy a Spanish SIM card for your cell phone, or even a cheap Spanish cell phone with a top-up SIM.

2 Match and repeat (4 minutes)

Match the numbered items to the Spanish in the panel on the left, then test yourself.

1 el cargador
el kargador

2 el teléfono
el telefonoh

3 el contestador automático
el kontestador aootomateekoh

4 los auriculares
los aooreekoolares

5 el móvil
el mobeel

6 la tarjeta SIM
lah tarhetah seem

telephone **2**

charger **1**

headphones **4**

5 mobile

3 In conversation (4 minutes)

Dígame, Susana Castillo al habla.
deegamay, soosanah kasteeyoh al ablah

Hello. Susana Castillo speaking.

Buenos días. Quisiera hablar con Julián López, por favor.
bwenos deeyas. keesyair-ah ablar kon hooleean lopeth, por fabor

Hello. I'd like to speak to Julián López, please.

¿De parte de quién?
day partay day kee-en?

Who's calling?

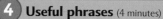

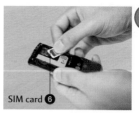

SIM card ❻

Quisiera comprar una tarjeta SIM.
keesyairah komprar oonah tarhetah seem
I'd like to buy a SIM card.

❸ answering machine

4 Useful phrases (4 minutes)

Practice these phrases and then test yourself using the cover flap.

I'd like the number for Juan.

Quisiera el número de Juan.
keesyairah el noomeroh dey hosay

I'd like to speak to María Alfaro.

Quisiera hablar con María Alfaro.
keesyairah ablar kon mareeah alfaroh

Can I leave a message?

¿Puedo dejar un mensaje?
pwedoh dehar oon mensahay

Sorry, I have the wrong number.

Perdone, me he equivocado de número.
perdonay, may ay ekeebokadoh day noomeroh

5 Say it (2 minutes)

I'd like to speak to Mr. Girona.

Can I leave a message for Antonio?

José Ortega, de Imprentas Lacuesta.
hosay ortegah, day eemprentas lakwestah

José Ortega of Lacuesta Printers.

Lo siento. La línea está comunicando.
loh syaintoh. lah leeneah estah komooneekandoh

I'm sorry. The line is busy.

¿Le puede decir que me llame, por favor?
lay pweday detheer kay may yamay, por fabor

Can you ask him to call me, please?

REPASE Y REPITA
Review and repeat

Respuestas
Answers (Cover with flap)

1 Sums

❶ **dieciséis**
deeaythee<u>say</u>ees

❷ **treinta y nueve**
<u>trey</u>ntah ee <u>nwe</u>bay

❸ **cincuenta y tres**
theen<u>kwen</u>tah ee tres

❹ **setenta y cuatro**
se<u>ten</u>tah ee <u>kwa</u>troh

❺ **noventa y nueve**
no<u>ben</u>tah ee <u>nwe</u>bay

1 Sums (4 minutes)

Say the answers
to these sums out
loud in Spanish.
Then check to see if
you remembered
correctly.

❶ 10 + 6 = ?
❷ 14 + 25 = ?
❸ 66 - 13 = ?
❹ 40 + 34 = ?
❺ 90 + 9 = ?

3 Telephones (3 minutes)

What are the numbered
items in Spanish?

cell phone ❶

❷ SIM card

2 I want...

❶ **Quiere**
<u>kyai</u>ray

❷ **quiere**
<u>kyai</u>ray

❸ **queremos**
ke<u>ray</u>mos

❹ **quieres**
<u>kyai</u>res

❺ **quieren**
<u>kyai</u>ren

❻ **quiero**
<u>kyai</u>roh

2 I want... (3 minutes)

Fill in the blanks with the
correct form of **querer**
(*to want*).

❶ ¿ _____ usted un café?

❷ Ella _____ ir de
vacaciones.

❸ Nosotros _____ una
mesa para tres.

❹ Tú _____ una cerveza.

❺ Ellos _____ una mesa
para dos.

❻ Yo _____ caramelos.

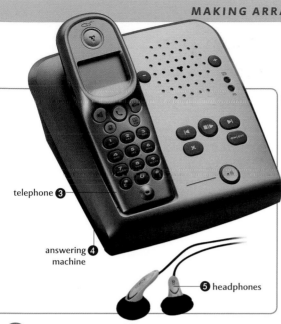

telephone **3**

answering **4**
machine

5 headphones

Respuestas
Answers (Cover with flap)

3 Telephones

1 el móvil
el mobeel

2 la tarjeta SIM
lah tarhetah seem

3 el teléfono
el telefonoh

4 el contestador
automático
*el kontestador
aootomateekoh*

5 los auriculares
los aooreekoolares

---

4 When? (2 minutes)

What do these sentences mean?

1 Tengo una cita el lunes veinte de mayo.

2 Mi cumpleaños es en septiembre.

3 Hoy es domingo.

4 No trabajo en agosto.

4 When?

1 I have a meeting on Monday, May 20th.
2 My birthday is in September.
3 Today is Sunday.
4 I don't work in August.

---

5 Time (3 minutes)

Say these times in Spanish.

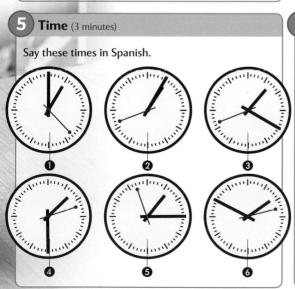

1 **2** **3**

4 **5** **6**

5 Time

1 la una
lah oonah

2 la una y cinco
la oonah ee theenkoh

3 la una y veinte
lah oonah ee beyntay

4 la una y media
lah oonah ee medee-ah

5 la una y cuarto
lah oonah ee kwartoh

6 las dos menos diez
las dos menos dyeth

1 Warm up (1 minute)

Count to 100 in tens.
(pp.10-11, pp.30-1)

Ask "What time is it?"
(pp.30-1)

Say "One-thirty."
(pp.30-1)

EN LA OFICINA DE BILLETES
At the ticket office

In Spain, commuter trains are very economical, clean, and efficient. Long-distance trains still offer smoking and nonsmoking carriages, and the prices vary depending on what day you travel, blue days being the cheapest.

2 Words to remember (3 minutes)

Learn these words and then test yourself.

la estación *lah estathyon*	(train) station
la terminal *lah termeenal*	(bus) station
el billete *el beeyetay*	ticket
de ida *day eedah*	one-way
de ida y vuelta *day eedah ee bweltah*	round-trip
de primera *day preemerah*	first class
de segunda *day segoondah*	second class
el descuento *el deskwentoh*	discount

el pasajero
el pasahairoh
passenger

la señal
lah senyal
sign

La estación está llena de gente.
lah estathyon estah yenah day hentay
The station is crowded.

3 In conversation (4 minutes)

Dos billetes para Bilbao, por favor.
dos beeyetes parah beebaoh, por fabor

Two tickets to Bilbao, please.

¿De ida y vuelta?
day eedah y bweltah

Round-trip?

Sí. ¿Necesito reservar asiento?
see. netheseetoh rreseerbar asyaintoh

Yes. Do I need to reserve seats?

4 Useful phrases (5 minutes)

Mi tren va con retraso.
mee tren bah kon rretrasoh
My train is late.

el tren	el andén
el tren	*el anden*
train	platform

Learn these phrases and then test yourself using the cover flap.

How much is a ticket to Madrid?	**¿Cuánto cuesta un billete para Madrid?** *kwantoh kwaystah oon beeyetay parah madreed*
Can I pay by credit card?	**¿Puedo pagar con tarjeta de crédito?** *pwedoh pagar kon tarhetah day kredeetoh*
Do I have to change trains?	**¿Tengo que cambiar?** *tengoh kay kambee-ar*
Which platform does the train leave from?	**¿De qué andén sale el tren?** *day kay anden salay el tren*
Are there any discounts?	**¿Hay algún descuento?** *ah-ee algoon deskwentoh*
What time does the train to Gijón leave?	**¿A qué hora sale el tren para Gijón?** *ah kay orah salay el tren parah geehon*

5 Say it (2 minutes)

Which platform does the train to Madrid leave from?

Three round-trip tickets to Murcia, please.

Cultural tip Most train stations have automatic ticket machines that will often also take credit cards.

No hace falta. Cuarenta euros, por favor.
noh ahthay faltah. kwarentah eh-ooros, por fabor

That's not necessary. Forty euros, please.

¿Aceptan tarjetas de crédito?
ahtheptan tarhetas day kredeetoh

Do you take credit cards?

Si. El tren sale del andén cinco.
see. el tren salay del anden theenkoh

Yes. The train leaves from platform five.

1 **Warm up** (1 minute)

What is "train" in Spanish? (pp.38-9)

What does "¿De qué andén sale el tren?" mean? (pp.38-9)

Ask "When are you free?" (pp.32-3)

IR Y COGER
To go and to take

The verbs **ir** (to go) and **coger** (to take) allow you to create many useful sentences. Note that **coger** can also mean to catch: **coger una pelota** (to catch a ball), **coger un resfriado** (to catch a cold); to grab: **coger a alguien** (to grab someone); and to hold: **coger a un bebé** (to hold a baby).

2 **Ir: to go** (6 minutes)

Spanish uses the same form of **ir** for both I go and I am going: **voy a Madrid** (I am going to Madrid/I go to Madrid). The same is true of other verbs—for example, **cojo el metro** (I am taking the metro/I take the metro).

yo voy *yoh boy*	I go
tú vas/usted va *too bas/oosted bah*	you go (informal/formal singular)
él/ella va *el/eh-yah bah*	he/she goes
nosotros(-as) vamos *nosotros(-as) bamos*	we go
vosotros(-as) vais/ ustedes van *bosotros/-as baees/ oostedes ban*	you go (informal/formal plural)
ellos/ellas van *eh-yos/eh-yas ban*	they go
¿A dónde vas? *ah donday bas*	Where are you going?
Voy a Madrid. *boy ah madreed*	I am going to Madrid.

Voy a la Plaza de España.
boy ah lah plathah day espanyah
I am going to the Plaza de España.

Conversational tip You may have noticed that **de** (of) combines with **el** to produce **del** as in **Museo del Prado** (literally, museum of the Prado); **el menú del día** (menu of the day). In the same way, **a** (to) combines with **el** to produce **al**: **Voy al museo** (I'm going to the museum). With feminine and plural words, **de** remains separate from **la**, **los**, and **las**.

3 Coger: to take (6 minutes)

Say the present tense of **coger** (*to take*) aloud. Use the cover flap to test yourself. When you are confident, practice the sentences below.

yo cojo *yoh kohoh*	I take
tú coges/usted coge *too kohes/oosted kohay*	you take (informal/ formal singular)
él/ella coge *el/eh-yah kohay*	he/she takes
nosotros(-as) cogemos *nosotros(-as) kohaymos*	we take
vosotros(-as) cogéis/ ustedes cogen *bosotros(-as) kohe-ees/ oostedes kohen*	you take (informal/ formal plural)
ellos/ellas cogen *eh-yos/eh-yas kohen*	they take

Yo cojo el metro todos los días.
yoh kohoh el metroh todos los deeyas
I take the metro every day.

No quiero coger un taxi. *noh kyairoh koher oon taksee*	I don't want to take a taxi.
Coja la primera a la izquierda. *kohah lah preemerah ah lah eethkyairdah*	Take the first left.

4 Put into practice (2 minutes)

Cover the text on the right and complete the dialogue in Spanish.

¿A dónde va?
ah donday bah

Where are you going?

Say: I'm going to the Puerta del Sol.

Voy a la Puerta del Sol.
boy ah lah pwertah del sol

¿Quiere coger el autobús?
kyairay koher el aootoboos

Do you want to take the bus?

Say: No, I want to go by metro.

No, quiero ir en metro.
noh, kyairoh eer en metroh

1 Warm up (1 minute)

Say "I don't want to take a taxi." (pp.40-1)

Ask "Where are you going?" (pp.40-1)

Say "80" and "40." (pp.30-1)

TAXI, AUTOBÚS, Y METRO
Taxi, bus, and metro

The metro and some buses operate a ticket system where you have to validate your tickets in a machine. There's a standard fare per ride, but you can also buy a **metrobús**, a book of 10 tickets for both buses and metro.

2 Words to remember (4 minutes)

Familiarize yourself with these words.

el autobús *el aootoboos*	bus
la taquilla *lah takeeyah*	ticket office
la estación de metro *lah estathyon day metroh*	metro station
la parada de autobús *lah paradah day aootoboos*	bus stop
la tarifa *lah tareefah*	fare
el taxi *el taksee*	taxi
la parada de taxis *lah paradah day taksees*	taxi stand

¿Para aquí el 17?
parah ahkee el deeaytheeseeaytay
Does the route 17 bus stop here?

3 In conversation: taxi (2 minutes)

A la Plaza de España, por favor.
ah lah plathah day espanyah, por fabor

Plaza de España, please.

Sí, de acuerdo, señor.
see, day akwairdo, senyor

Yes, certainly, sir.

¿Me puede dejar aquí, por favor?
may pweday dehar ahkee, por fabor

Can you drop me here, please?

4 Useful phrases (4 minutes)

Practice these phrases and then test yourself using the cover flap.

I'd like a taxi to go to the Prado.	**Quisiera un taxi para ir al Prado.**
	keesyairah oon taksee parah eer al prado
When is the next bus?	**¿Cuándo sale el próximo autobús?**
	kwandoh salay el prokseemoh aootoboos
How do you get to the museum?	**¿Cómo se va al museo?**
	komoh say bah al moosayoh
How long is the trip?	**¿Cuánto dura el viaje?**
	kwantoh doorah el beeahay
Please wait for me.	**Espéreme, por favor.**
	esperemay, por fabor

Cultural tip Metro lines in Madrid are known by numbers and the names of the first and last stations. Look for the relevant end station. The Madrid metro runs every day between 6:00 am and 2:00 am.

6 Say it (2 minutes)

Do you go near the train station?

Do you go near the Prado?

When is the next bus to Barcelona?

5 In conversation: bus (2 minutes)

¿Pasa cerca del museo?
pasah therkah del moosayoh

Do you go near the museum?

Sí. Son 80 céntimos.
see. son ochentah thenteemos

Yes. That's 80 cents.

Avíseme cuando lleguemos.
abeesemay kwandoh yeghemos

Tell me when we arrive.

EN LA CARRETERA
On the road

1 Warm up (1 minute)

How do you say "I have..."? (pp.14-15)

Say "my father," "my sister," and "my parents." (pp.10-11, pp.12-13)

Say "I'm going to Madrid." (pp.40-1)

Spanish **autopistas** (*toll highways*) are fast but can be quite expensive. You will find signs for **el peaje** (*toll payment stations*). These have multiple lanes. Make sure you enter a green lane that allows payment by cash or credit card. Some lanes are for pass-holders or trucks only.

2 Match and repeat (4 minutes)

Match the numbered items to the list on the left, then test yourself.

1 el maletero
el malaytairoh

2 el parabrisas
el parabreesas

3 el capó
el kapoh

4 la rueda
lah rwedah

5 el neumático
el ne-oomateekoh

6 la puerta
lah pwertah

7 los faros
los faros

8 el parachoques
el parachokes

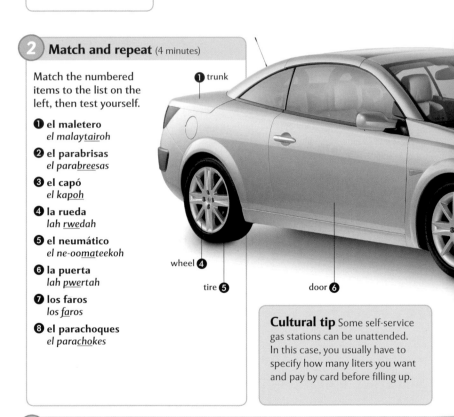

1 trunk

wheel **4**

tire **5**

door **6**

Cultural tip Some self-service gas stations can be unattended. In this case, you usually have to specify how many liters you want and pay by card before filling up.

3 Road features (2 minutes)

la rotonda
lah rrotonduh

roundabout

el semáforo
el semaforoh

traffic lights

el cruce
el kroothay

intersection

4 Useful phrases (4 minutes)

Learn these phrases and then test yourself using the cover flap.

The turn signal doesn't work	**El intermitente no funciona.** *el intairmeetaintay noh foonthyonah*
Fill it up, please.	**Lleno, por favor.** *yennoh, por fabor*

➋ windshield

➌ hood

headlights ➐   ➑ bumper

5 Words to remember (3 minutes)

Familiarize yourself with these words, then test yourself using the cover flap.

gasoline	**la gasolina** *lah gasoleenah*
diesel	**el gasoil** *el gasoil*
oil	**el aceite** *el ah-thayeetay*
engine	**el motor** *el motor*
gearbox	**la caja de cambios** *lah kahah day kambyos*
turn signal	**el intermitente** *el intairmeetaintay*
flat tire	**la rueda pinchada** *lah rwaydah peenchadah*
exhaust	**el tubo de escape** *el tooboh day eskapay*
driver's license	**el carné de conducir** *el karnay day kondootheer*

6 Say it (1 minutes)

There's something wrong with my engine.

I have a flat tire.

la autopista
lah aootopeestah

highway/expressway

la autopista de peaje
lah aootopeestah day pyahay

toll highway

el atasco de tráfico
el ataskoh day trafeekoh

traffic jam

REPASE Y REPITA
Review and repeat

1 Transport

❶ el autobús
el aootoboos

❷ el taxi
el taksee

❸ el coche
el kochay

❹ la bicicleta
lah beetheekletah

❺ el metro
el metroh

1 Transportation (3 minutes)

Name these forms of
transport in Spanish.

bus ❶

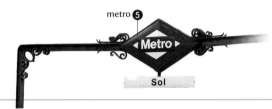

metro ❺

2 Go and take

❶ ir
eer

❷ cojo
kohoh

❸ va
bah

❹ vamos
bamos

❺ cogen
kohen

❻ voy
boy

2 Go and take (4 minutes)

Use the correct form of the verb in brackets.

❶ Quiero ____ a la estación. (ir)

❷ Yo ____ el metro. (coger)

❸ ¿A dónde ____ usted? (ir)

❸ Nosotros ____ al Museo del Prado. (ir)

❺ Ellos ____ (coger) un taxi.

❻ Yo ____ (ir) a Madrid.

① taxi

③ car

④ bicycle

③ You (4 minutes)

Use the correct form for **usted** or **tú** in each sentence.

① You are in a café. Ask "Do you have churros?"

② You are with a friend. Ask "Do you want a beer?"

③ A visitor approaches you at your company's reception desk. Ask "Do you have an ppointment?"

④ You are on the bus. Ask "Do you go near the station?"

⑤ Ask your friend where she's going tomorrow.

Respuestas
Answers (Cover with flap)

③ You

① ¿Tiene churros?
_tye_nay _choo_rros

② ¿Quieres una cerveza?
_kyaires oo_nah thair_bay_thah

③ ¿Tiene una cita?
_tye_nay _oo_nah _thee_tah

④ ¿Pasa cerca de la estación?
_pasah _ther_kah day lah estath_yon

⑤ ¿A dónde vas mañana?
_ah _donday bas _manyanah

④ Tickets (4 minutes)

You're buying tickets at a train station. Follow the conversation, replying in Spanish following the numbered English prompts.

¿Qué desea?
① I'd like two tickets to Sevilla.

¿De ida o de ida y vuelta?
② Round-trip, please.

Muy bien. Cincuenta euros, por favor.
③ What time does the train leave?

A las tres y diez.
④ What platform does the train leave from?

Andén número siete.
⑤ Thank you very much. Goodbye.

④ Tickets

① Quisiera dos billetes para Sevilla.
kees_yai_rah dos bee_yetes _parah sebee_eyah

② De ida y vuelta, por favor.
day _ee_dah ee _bwel_tah, por fa_bor

③ ¿A qué hora sale el tren?
ah kay _orah _salay el tren

④ ¿De qué andén sale el tren?
day kay an_den _salay el tren

⑤ Muchas gracias. Adiós.
_moochas _grathyas. addy-_os

EN LA CIUDAD
Around town

1 Warm up (1 minute)

Ask "How do you get to the museum?" (pp.42-3)

Say "I want to take the metro" and "I don't want to take a taxi." (pp.40-1)

Note that the Spanish word **museo** (*museum*) also means art gallery when it's a public building in which works of art are exhibited; **galería de arte** usually refers to a shop that sells works of art. Be careful, too, not to confuse **librería** (*bookshop* or *bookshelf*) and **biblioteca** (*library*).

2 Match and repeat (4 minutes)

Match the numbered locations to the words in the panel.

❶ **el ayuntamiento**
el ahyoonta-myaintoh

❷ **el puente**
el pwentay

❸ **el centro**
el thentroh

❹ **la iglesia**
lah eegleseeah

❺ **la plaza**
lah plathah

❻ **el aparcamiento**
el aparka-myaintoh

❼ **la biblioteca**
lah bibleeotekah

❽ **el museo**
el moosayoh

❶ town hall   church ❹

downtown ❸

❺ square

3 Words to remember (3 minutes)

Familiarize yourself with these words and test yourself using the cover flap.

la gasolinera *lah gasoleenerah*	gas station
la oficina de información turística *lah ohfeetheenah day eenformathyon tooreesteekah*	tourist information
la piscina municipal *lah pistheenah mooneetheepal*	public swimming pool

❼ library

Conversational tip In Spanish there are two ways of saying *am*, *is*, or *are*. You have already learned the verb **ser** (p.14): **soy inglés** (*I am English*); **es vegetariano** (*he is vegetarian*). When talking about where something is, you need to use a different verb: **estar**. The most important forms of this verb are: **estoy** (*I am*), **está** (*he/she/it is*), and **están** (*they are*): **¿Dónde están lla iglesia?** (*Where is the church?*); **El café no está lejos**. (*The café isn't far.*)

4 Useful phrases (4 minutes)

La catedral está en el centro.
lah katedral estah en el thentroh
The cathedral is downtown.

Practice these phrases and then test yourself using the cover flap.

Is there an art gallery in town?	**¿Hay algún museo de arte en la ciudad?** *ah-ee algoon moosayoh day artay en lah thyoodad*
Is it far from here?	**¿Está lejos de aquí?** *estah lehos day ahkee*
There is a swimming pool near the bridge.	**Hay una piscina cerca del puente.** *ah-ee oonah peestheenah therkah del pwentay*

5 Put into practice (3 minutes)

bridge ❷

parking lot ❻

museum ❽

Join in this conversation. Read the Spanish on the left and follow the instructions to make your reply. Then test yourself.

¿Le puedo ayudar? *lay pwedoh ahyoodar* Can I help you? Ask: Is there a library in town?	**¿Hay alguna biblioteca en la ciudad?** *ah-ee algoonah beebleeotekah en lah thyoodad*
No, pero hay un museo. *noh, peroh ah-ee oon moosayoh* No, but there's a museum. Ask: How do I get to the museum?	**¿Cómo se va al museo?** *komoh say bah al moosayoh*
Está por allí. *estah por ahyee* It's over there. Say: Thank you very much.	**Muchas gracias.** *moochas grathyas*

How do you say "near
the station"? (pp.42–3)

Say "Take the first left."
(pp.40–1)

Ask "Where are you
going?" (pp.40–1)

LAS DIRECCIONES
Directions

You'll often be able to find a **plano de la ciudad**
(*town map*) in the downtown area, usually near the
town hall or tourist office. In the older parts of
Spanish towns there are often narrow streets, in
which you will usually find a one-way system
in operation. Parking is usually restricted.

2 **Useful phrases** (4 minutes)

Learn these phrases and then test yourself.

Tuerza a la izquierda/ derecha. *twerthah ah lah eethkyairdah/derechah*	Turn left/right.
todo recto *todoh rrektoh*	straight on
¿Cómo se va a la piscina? *komoh say bah ah lah peestheenah*	How do I get to the swimming pool?
la primera a la derecha *lah preemerah ah lah derechah*	first right
la segunda a la izquierda *lah segoondah ah lah eethkyairdah*	second left

el bloque de oficinas
el blokay day ohfeetheenas
office block

la fuente
lah fwentay
fountain

3 **In conversation** (4 minutes)

**¿Hay un restaurante en
la ciudad?**
*ah-ee oon restaoorantay
en la thyoodad*

Is there a
restaurant in town?

Sí, cerca de la estación.
*see, therkah day lah
estathyon*

Yes, near the station.

¿Cómo se va a la estación?
*komoh say bah ah
lah estathyon*

How do I get to the station?

4 Words to remember (4 minutes)

Me he perdido.
may eh perdeedoh
I'm lost.

Familiarize yourself with these words and test yourself using the cover flap.

traffic lights	**el semáforo** *el semaforoh*
corner	**la esquina** *lah eskeenah*
street/road	**la calle** *lah kayay*
main road	**la calle principal** *lah kayay preentheepal*
at the end of the street	**al final de la calle** *al feenal day lah kayay*
map	**el plano** *el planoh*
overpass	**el paso elevado** *el pasoh elebadoh*
across from	**enfrente de** *enfrentay day*

el centro deportivo
el thentroh deporteeboh
gym

la zona peatonal
lah thonah pe-ahtonal
pedestrian zone

¿Dondé estamos?
donday estamos
Where are we?

5 Say it (2 minutes)

Turn right at the end of the street.

Turn left across from the museum.

It's ten minutes by bus.

Tuerza a la izquierda en el semáforo.
twerthah ah lah eethkyairdah en el semaforoh

Turn left at the traffic lights.

¿Está lejos?
estah lehos

Is it far?

No, cinco minutos andando.
noh, theenkoh meenootos andandoh

No, it's five minutes on foot.

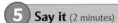

1 Warm up (1 minute)

Say the days of the week in Spanish. (pp.28–9)

How do you say "six o'clock"? (pp.30–1)

Ask "What time is it?" (pp.30–1)

EL TURISMO
Sightseeing

Most national museums and art galleries close on Mondays and public holidays. Although stores are normally closed on Sundays, many will open in tourist areas. It is not unusual for public buildings and shops to close at lunchtime, between 1:30 and 4:30 pm.

2 Words to remember (4 minutes)

Familiarize yourself with these words and test yourself using the cover flap.

la guía *lah gheeah*	guidebook
la entrada *lah entradah*	admission ticket
el horario de apertura *el oraryoh day apertoorah*	opening times
el día festivo *el deeyah festeevoh*	public holiday
entrada libre *entradah leebray*	free admission

la visita con guía
lah beeseetah kon gheeah
guided tour

Cultural tip If a public holiday falls on a Thursday or a Tuesday, the Spanish will often **hacer puente** (do a bridge)—in other words, take Friday or Monday off to make a long weekend.

3 In conversation (3 minutes)

¿Abren esta tarde?
ahbren estah tarday

Are you open
this afternoon?

**Sí, pero cerramos a
las cuatro.**
*see, peroh therramos ah las
kwatroh*

Yes, but we close at
four o'clock.

**¿Tienen acceso para sillas
de ruedas?**
*tyenen akthesoh parah
seeyas day rwedas*

Do you have access
for wheelchairs?

4 Useful phrases (3 minutes)

Practice these phrases and then test yourself using the cover flap.

What time do you open/close?	**¿A qué hora abre/cierra?** ah kay _orah_ _ah_bray/ thy_ai_rrah
Where are the restrooms?	**¿Dónde están los servicios?** _donday_ es_tan_ los ser_beeth_yos
Is there access for wheelchairs?	**¿Hay acceso para sillas de ruedas?** ah-ee ak_thes_oh _parah_ _see_yas day _rw_edas

5 Put into practice (4 minutes)

Cover the text on the right and complete the dialogue in Spanish.

Lo siento, el museo está cerrado. loh _syen_toh, el moo_say_oh es_tah_ ther_ra_doh	**¿Abren los martes?** _ah_bren los _martes_
Sorry. The museum is closed.	
Ask: Are you open on Tuesdays?	
Sí, pero cerramos temprano. see, _per_oh ther_ra_mos tem_pra_noh	**¿A qué hora?** ah kay _orah_
Yes, but we close early.	
Ask: At what time?	

Sí, el ascensor está allí.
see, el asthen_sor_ es_tah_ ah-_yee_

Yes, there's an elevator over there.

Gracias, quisiera cuatro entradas.
_grath_yas, kees_yair_ah _kwa_troh en_tra_das

Thank you, I'd like four admission tickets.

Aquí tiene, y la guía es gratis.
ah_kee_ _tye_nay, ee lah _ghee_ah es _gra_tees

Here you are, and the guidebook is free.

1 Warm up (1 minute)

Say "one-thirty."
(pp.30-1)

What's the Spanish for
"ticket"? (pp.38-9)

Say "I am going to New
York." (pp.40-1)

EN EL AEROPUERTO
At the airport

Although the airport environment is largely international, it is sometimes useful to be able to ask your way around the terminal in Spanish. It's a good idea to make sure you have a few coins when you arrive at the airport; you may need to pay for a luggage cart.

2 Words to remember (4 minutes)

Familiarize yourself with these words and test yourself using the cover flap.

la facturación *lah faktoorathyon*	check-in
las salidas *las saleedas*	departures
las llegadas *las yehgadas*	arrivals
la aduana *lah adwanah*	customs
el control de pasaportes *el kontrol day pasaportes*	passport control
la terminal *lah termeenal*	terminal
la puerta de embarque *lah pwertah day embarkay*	boarding gate

¿Cuál es la puerta de embarque para el vuelo veintitrés?
kwal es lah pwertah day embarkay parah el bweloh bayeenteetres
What is the boarding gate for flight 23?

3 Useful phrases (3 minutes)

Learn these phrases and then test yourself using the cover flap.

¿Sale a su hora el vuelo para Sevilla? *salay ah soo orah el bweloh parah seveeyah*	Is the flight to Seville on time?
No encuentro mi equipaje. *noh enkwentroh mee ehkeepahay*	I can't find my luggage.

4 Put into practice (3 minutes)

Join in this conversation. Read the Spanish on the left and follow the instructions to make your reply. Then test yourself by concealing the answers using the cover flap.

Hola, ¿le puedo ayudar?
o-lah, lay pwedoh ahyoodar

Hello, can I help you?

Ask: Is the flight to Madrid on time?

¿Sale a su hora el vuelo para Madrid?
salay ah soo orah el bweloh parah madreed

Sí señor.
see senyor

Yes sir.

Ask: What is the boarding gate?

¿Cuál es la puerta de embarque?
kwal es lah pwertah day embarkay

5 Match and repeat (4 minutes)

Match the numbered items to the Spanish words in the panel.

❶ **la tarjeta de embarque**
lah tarhetah day embarkay

❷ **el mostrador de facturación**
el mostrador day faktoorathyon

❸ **el billete**
el beeyehtay

❹ **el pasaporte**
el pasaportay

❺ **la maleta**
lah malaytah

❻ **el equipaje de mano**
el ehkeepahay day manoh

❼ **el carrito**
el karreetoh

boarding ❶ pass

check-in ❷ desk

ticket ❸

passport ❹

❼ cart

❺ suitcase   ❻ carry-on luggage

REPASE Y REPITA
Review and repeat

1 Places

❶ **el museo**
el moosayoh

❷ **el ayuntamiento**
el ahyoonta-myaintoh

❸ **el puente**
el pwentay

❹ **la biblioteca**
lah beeblee-ohtekah

❺ **el aparcamiento**
el ahparka-myaintoh

❻ **la catedral**
lah katedral

❼ **la plaza**
lah plathah

1 Places (4 minutes)

Name the numbered places in Spanish.

❶ museum

❷ town hall

❸ bridge

❹ library

❺ parking lot

❻ cathedral

square ❼

2 Car parts

❶ **el parabrisas**
el parabreesas

❷ **el intermitente**
el intairmee-taintay

❸ **el capó**
el kapoh

❹ **el neumático**
el ne-oomateekoh

❺ **la puerta**
lah pwertah

❻ **el parachoques**
el parachokes

2 Car parts (3 minutes)

Name these car parts in Spanish.

windshield ❶

❹ tire   ❺ door

3 Questions (4 minutes)

Ask the questions that match these answers.

❶ **El autobús sale a las ocho.**
el aootoboos salay ah las ochoh

❷ **El café es un euro cincuenta.**
el kafay es oon eh-ooro theenkwentah

❸ **No, no quiero vino.**
noh, noh kyairoh beenoh

❹ **El tren sale del andén cinco.**
el tren salay del anden theenkoh

❺ **Nosotros vamos a León.**
nosotros bamos ah leh-on

❻ **El próximo tren es dentro de quince minutos.**
el prokseemoh tren es dentroh day keenthay meenootos

3 Questions

❶ **¿A qué hora sale el autobús?**
ah kay orah salay el aootoboos

❷ **¿Cuánto es el café?**
kwantoh es el kafay

❸ **¿Quieres vino?**
kyaires beenoh

❹ **¿De qué andén sale el tren?**
day kay anden salay el tren

❺ **¿A dónde vais?**
ah donday baees

❻ **¿Cuándo es el próximo tren?**
kwandoh es el prokseemoh tren

❷ turn signal

❸ hood

❻ bumper

4 Verbs (4 minutes)

Choose the correct form of the verb in brackets to fill in the blanks.

❶ **Yo _____ inglés. (ser)**

❷ **Nosotros _____ el metro. (tomar)**

❸ **Ella _____ a Marbella. (ir)**

❹ **Él _____ casado. (estar)**

❺ **¿Tú _____ un té? (querer)**

❻ **¿Cuántos niños _____ usted? (tener)**

4 Verbs

❶ **soy**
soy

❷ **cogemos**
kohaymos

❸ **va**
bah

❹ **está**
estah

❺ **quieres**
kyaires

❻ **tiene**
tyenay

1 Warm up (1 minute)

Ask "Do you accept credit cards?" (pp.38–9)

Ask "How much is that?" (pp.18–19)

Ask "Do you have children?" (pp.10–11)

RESERVAR UNA HABITACIÓN
Booking a room

Types of accommodation in Spain include: **hotel**, categorized from one to five stars; **pensión**, a small family-run hotel; **hostal**, cheap and basic; and **parador**, state-owned hotels in historic properties or places of great beauty.

2 Useful phrases (3 minutes)

Practice these phrases and then test yourself by concealing the Spanish on the left using the cover flap.

¿El desayuno está incluido?
el desayoonoh estah inklooeedoh

Is breakfast included?

¿Aceptan animales de compañía?
atheptan aneemales day kompanyeeah

Do you accept pets?

¿Tienen servicio de habitaciones?
tyenen serbeethyoh day abeetathyones

Do you have room service?

¿A qué hora tengo que dejar la habitación?
ah kay orah tengoh kay dehar lah abeetathyon

What time do I have to check out?

3 In conversation (5 minutes)

¿Tiene habitaciones libres?
tyenay abeetathyones leebres

Do you have any vacancies?

Sí, una habitación doble.
see, oonah abeetathyon doblay

Yes, a double room.

¿Tiene una cuna?
tyenay oonah koonah

Do you have a crib?

4 Words to remember (4 minutes)

Familiarize yourself with these words and test yourself by concealing the Spanish on the right using the cover flap.

¿Tiene la habitación vistas al parque?
tyenay lah abeetathyon beestas al parkay
Does the room have a view over the park?

room	**la habitación** *lah abeetathyon*
single room	**la habitación individual** *lah abeetathyon indeebeedwal*
double room	**la habitación doble** *lah abeetathyon dubluy*
bathroom	**el cuarto de baño** *el kwartoh day banyoh*
shower	**la ducha** *lah doochah*
breakfast	**el desayuno** *el desayoonoh*
key	**la llave** *lah yabay*
balcony	**el balcón** *el balkon*
air-conditioning	**el aire acondicionado** *el ah-eeray akondeethyonadoh*

5 Say it (2 minutes)

Do you have a single room, please?

For six nights.

Is breakfast included?

Cultural tip Large hotels and paradors are generally the only types of hotels to offer breakfast, but you will generally be charged extra. If your accommodation doesn't provide breakfast, you'll usually find it easy to discover a bar or a café nearby where you can go for **café con leche** in the mornings.

Sí, claro. ¿Cuántas noches?
see, klaroh. kwantas noches

Yes, of course. How many nights?

Para tres noches.
parah tres noches

For three nights.

Muy bien. Aquí tiene la llave.
mwee byen. ahkee tyenay lah yabay

Fine. Here's the key.

1 Warm up (1 minute)

Say "Is there...?" and
"There isn't...". (pp.48-9)

What does "¿Le puedo
ayudar?" mean? (pp.54-5)

EN EL HOTEL
In the hotel

Although rooms in larger hotels almost always
have private bathrooms, there are still some
pensiones and **hostales** where you will have
to share bathroom facilities and in which towels
are not supplied. It is always advisable to check
what is provided when you make reservations.

2 Match and repeat (6 minutes)

Match the numbered items in this hotel bedroom with the
Spanish text in the panel and test yourself using the cover flap.

❶ **la mesilla de noche**
*lah meseeyah day
nochay*

❷ **la lámpara**
lah lamparah

❸ **el minibar**
el meeneebar

❹ **las cortinas**
las korteenas

❺ **el sofá**
el sofah

❻ **la almohada**
lah almoh-ahdah

❼ **el cojín**
el koheen

❽ **la cama**
lah kamah

❾ **la colcha**
lah kolchah

❿ **la manta**
lah mantah

❹ curtains

❺ sofa

❶ nightstand

❸ mini bar

❷ lamp

❽ bed

❾ bedspread

❻ pillow   ❼ cushion   ❿ blanket

Cultural tip When you arrive in your double room, you will
usually see one long pillow instead of two individual ones on
the bed. This is the usual pillow for a double bed (**cama de
matrimonio** or *marriage bed*). If you don't want to share your
bed or pillow, you'll have to ask for **una habitación doble con
dos camas** (*a double room with two beds*) to get a twin room.

3 Useful phrases (5 minutes)

Practice these phrases and then test yourself using the cover flap.

The room is too cold/hot. **Hace demasiado frío/ calor en la habitación.**
ahthay daymasyahdoh freeoh/kalor en lah abeetathyon

There are no towels. **No hay toallas.**
noh ah-ee toh-ahyas

I need some soap. **Necesito jabón.**
netheseetoh habon

The shower doesn't work. **La ducha no funciona.**
lah doochah noh foonthyonah

The elevator is broken. **El ascensor está roto.**
el asthensor estah rrotoh

4 Put into practice (3 minutes)

Practice these phrases and then complete the dialogue in Spanish.

¿Le atienden? **Necesito almohadas.**
lay atyainden *netheseetoh almoh-ahdas*

Can I help you?

Say: I need some pillows.

La camarera se las llevará. **Y la televisión no**
lah kamarairah say **funciona.**
las yebarah *ee lah telebeesyon noh foonthyonah*

The maid will bring some.

Say: And the TV doesn't work.

1 **Warm up** (1 minute)

How do you ask
"Can I?" (pp.34-5)

Say "The elevator is
broken." (pp.60-1)

Say "I need some towels."
(pp.60-1)

EN EL CÁMPING
At the campground

Camping is very popular in Spain. The country's
numerous campgrounds are well organized and
operate on a star system. The local tourist information
office will be able to offer a list of campgrounds in
the area with their ratings. It is advisable to book
in advance during the summer months.

2 **Useful phrases** (3 minutes)

Learn these phrases and then test
yourself by concealing the Spanish
with the cover flap.

¿Puedo alquilar una bicicleta? _pwedoh alkeelar oonah beetheekletah_	Can I rent a bicycle?
¿Es el agua potable? _es el ahgwah potablay_	Is this drinking water?
¿Se permiten hogueras? _say permeeten ohgheras_	Are campfires allowed?
Las radios están prohibidas. _las rradyos estan proheebeedas_	Radios are forbidden.

¿Dónde está el grifo?
donday estah el greefoh
Where is the faucet?

la oficina
lah ofeetheenah
office

**el contenedor de
la basura**
_el kontenedor day
lah basoorah_
trash can

el doble techo
el doblay taychoh
flysheet

3 **In conversation** (5 minutes)

**Necesito una plaza para
tres noches.**
_netheseetoh oonah plathah
parah tres noches_

I need a site for
three nights.

**Hay una cerca de
la piscina.**
_ah-ee oonah therkah day
lah peestheenah_

There's one near the
swimming pool.

**¿Cuánto cuesta para una
roulotte?**
_kwantoh kwestah parah
oonah rroolot_

How much is it for
a camper?

5 Say it (2 minutes)

I need a site for four nights.

Can I rent a tent?

Where's the electrical hookup?

4 Words to remember (4 minutes)

Learn these words and then test yourself using the cover flap.

campground	**el cámping** — el kampeen
tent	**la tienda** — lah tyendah
camper trailer	**la roulotte** — lah rroolot
camper van	**la autocaravana** — la ah-ootokarabanah
site	**la plaza** — lah plathah
campfire	**la hoguera** — lah ohgherah
drinking water	**el agua potable** — el ahgwah potablay
garbage	**la basura** — lah basoorah
stove fuel	**el camping-gas** — el kampeen gas
showers	**las duchas** — las doochas
sleeping bag	**el saco de dormir** — el sakoh day dormeer
air mattress	**la colchoneta** — lah kolchonetah
groundsheet	**el suelo aislante** — el sweloh ah-eeslantay

los aseos — los asayos — restrooms

el punto de luz — el poontoh day looth — electrical hookup

la cuerda — lah kwerdah — guy rope

la clavija — la klabeehah — tent peg

Cincuenta euros. Una noche por adelantado. — theenkwentah eh-ooros. oonah nochay por adelantadoh

Fifty euros. One night in advance.

¿Puedo alquilar una barbacoa? — pwedoh alkeelar oonah barbakoh-ah

Can I rent a barbecue grill?

Sí, pero tiene que dejar una señal. — see, peroh tyenay kay dehar oonah senyal

Yes, but you must pay a deposit.

How do you say "hot" and "cold"? (pp.60-1)

What is the Spanish for "room," "bed," and "pillow"? (pp.60-1)

DESCRIPCIONES
Descriptions

Adjectives are words used to describe things. In Spanish you generally put the adjective after the thing it describes in the same gender and number: **una bebida fría** (*a cold drink*, feminine singular); **un café frío** (*a cold coffee*, masculine singular); **dos bebidas frías** (*two cold drinks*, feminine plural).

2 **Words to remember** (7 minutes)

Adjectives change depending on whether the thing described is masculine **el** or feminine **la**. Generally, a final **o** changes to **a** in the feminine, but if the adjective ends with **e** such as **grande** it doesn't change for the feminine. For the plural, just add an **s**.

duro/dura *dooroh/doorah*	hard
blando/blanda *blandoh/blandah*	soft
caliente *kalyaintay*	hot
frío/fría *freeoh/freeah*	cold
grande *granday*	big
pequeño/pequeña *pekenyoh/pekenyah*	small
bonito/bonita *boneetoh/boneetah*	beautiful
feo/fea *feh-oh/feh-ah*	ugly
ruidoso/ruidosa *rrweedosoh/rrweedosah*	noisy
tranquilo/tranquila *trankeeloh/trankeelah*	quiet
bueno/buena *bwenoh/bwenah*	good
malo/mala *maloh/malah*	bad
lento/lenta *lentoh/lentah*	slow
rápido/rápida *rrapeedoh/rrapeedah*	fast

las montañas altas
las montanyas altas
high mountains

la tienda pequeña
lah tyaindah pekenyah
small shop

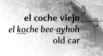

el coche viejo
el koche bee-ayhoh
old car

El pueblo es muy bonito.
el pwebloh es mwee boneetoh
The village is very beautiful.

la calle tranquila
lah kayay trankeelah
quiet road

3 Useful phrases (4 minutes)

Learn these phrases. Note that you can emphasize a description by using **muy** (*very*), **demasiado** (*too*), or **más** (*more*) before the adjective.

This coffee is cold.	**Este café está frío.** *estay kafay estah <u>free</u>-oh*
My room is very noisy.	**Mi habitación es muy ruidosa.** *mee abeeta<u>thyon</u> es mwee rrwee<u>dos</u>ah*
My car is too small.	**Mi coche es demasiado pequeño.** *mee <u>ko</u>che es dema<u>syah</u>doh pe<u>ke</u>nyoh*
I need a softer bed.	**Necesito una cama más blanda.** *nethe<u>see</u>toh <u>oo</u>nah <u>ka</u>mah mas <u>blan</u>dah*

4 Put into practice (3 minutes)

Join in this conversation. Cover up the text on the right and complete the dialogue in Spanish. Check and repeat if necessary.

Ésta es la habitación.
<u>es</u>tah es lah abeeta<u>thyon</u>
This is the bedroom.
Say: The view is very beautiful.

La vista es muy bonita.
lah <u>bees</u>tah es mwee bo<u>nee</u>tah

El cuarto de baño está por ahí.
el <u>kwar</u>toh day <u>ban</u>yoh es<u>tah</u> por ah-<u>ee</u>
The bathroom is over there.
Say: It is too small.

Es demasiado pequeño.
es dema<u>syah</u>doh pe<u>ke</u>nyoh

No tenemos otra.
noh te<u>nay</u>mos <u>o</u>trah
We don't have another one.
Say: It doesn't matter. We'll take the room.

No importa. Nos quedamos con la habitación.
noh im<u>por</u>tah. nos ke<u>da</u>mos kon lah abeeta<u>thyon</u>

REPASE Y REPITA
Review and repeat

1 Descriptions

❶ caliente
kalyaintay

❷ pequeña
pekenyah

❸ frío
free-oh

❹ grande
granday

❺ tranquila
trankeelah

1 Descriptions (3 minutes)

Put the word in brackets into Spanish. Use the correct masculine or feminine form.

❶ El agua está demasiado _____. (hot)

❷ La cama es muy _____. (small)

❸ El café está _____. (cold)

❹ Este cuarto de baño es más _____. (big)

❺ Quisiera una habitación más _____. (quiet)

2 Campground

❶ el punto de luz
el poontoh day looth

❷ la tienda
lah tyaindah

❸ el contenedor de la basura
el kontenedor day lah basoorah

❹ la cuerda
lah kwerdah

❺ los aseos
los asayos

❻ la roulotte
lah rroolot

2 Campground (3 minutes)

Name these items you might find in a campground.

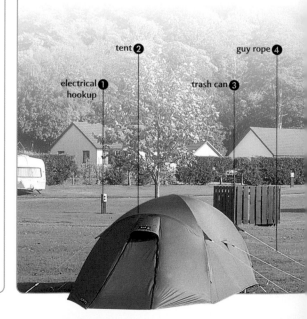

electrical ❶ hookup

tent ❷

trash can ❸

guy rope ❹

3 At the hotel (4 minutes)

You are booking a room in a hotel. Follow the conversation, replying in Spanish where you can see the English prompts.

¿Qué desean?
1 Do you have any vacancies?

Sí, una habitación doble.
2 Do you accept pets?

Sí. ¿Cuántas noches?
3 Three nights.

Son ciento cuarenta euros.
4 Is breakfast included?

Sí. Aquí tiene la llave.
5 Thank you very much.

3 At the hotel

1 ¿Tiene habitaciones libres?
tyenay abeeta-thyones leebres

2 ¿Aceptan animales de compañía?
atheptan aneemales day kompanyeeah

3 Tres noches.
tres noches

4 ¿El desayuno está incluido?
el desayoonoh estah inklooeedoh

5 Muchas gracias.
moochas grathyas

4 Negatives (5 minutes)

Make these sentences negative using the verb in brackets.

1 Yo _____ hijos. (tener)
2 Ellos _____ a Madrid mañana. (ir)
3 Él _____ un café. (querer)
4 Yo _____ el metro. (coger)
5 La vista _____ muy bonita. (ser)

4 Negatives

1 no tengo
noh tengoh

2 no van
noh ban

3 no quiere
noh kyairay

4 no cojo
noh kohoh

5 no es
no es

5 restrooms
6 camper

1 Warm up (1 minute)

Ask "How do I get to the station?" (pp.50-1)

Say "Turn left at the traffic lights" and "The station is across from the café." (pp.50-1)

DE COMPRAS
Shopping

Small, traditional shops are still very common in Spain. But you can also find big supermarkets and shopping centers on the outskirts of cities. Local markets selling fresh, local produce can be found everywhere. Ask which day is market day at the **oficina de información turística** (*tourist office*).

2 Match and repeat (5 minutes)

Match the stores numbered 1 to 9 below and right to the Spanish in the panel. Then test yourself using the cover flap.

① **la panadería**
lah panadair<u>ee</u>ah

② **la pastelería**
lah pastaylair<u>ee</u>ah

③ **el estanco**
el es<u>tan</u>koh

④ **la carnicería**
lah karnee-thair<u>ee</u>ah

⑤ **la charcutería**
lah charkoo-tair<u>ee</u>ah

⑥ **la librería**
lah leebrair<u>ee</u>ah

⑦ **la pescadería**
lah peskadair<u>ee</u>ah

⑧ **la joyería**
la hoyer<u>ee</u>ah

⑨ **el banco**
el <u>ban</u>koh

① bread shop

② bakery

④ butcher

⑤ delicatessen

⑦ fishmonger

⑧ jeweler

Conversational tip If you want an everyday bar of soap or a tube of toothpaste, you need to go to a **droguería** (*drugstore*) rather than the **farmacia** (*pharmacy*). The **estanco** (*tobacconist*) is the place for all sorts of tobacco products and stamps. **Papelerías** cater for all your stationery needs. Most Spanish shops offer a free gift-wrapping service; you only need to ask: **¿Me lo envuelve para regalo?** (*May I have it gift-wrapped?*).

¿Dónde está la floristería?
donday estah lah floreestaireeah
Where is the florist?

3 Words to remember (4 minutes)

Familiarize yourself with these words and test
yourself using the cover flap.

hardware store	**la ferretería** *lah ferretaireeah*
antique shop	**el anticuario** *el anteekwareeoh*
hairdresser	**la peluquería** *lah pelookaireeah*
greengrocer	**la verdulería** *lah berdoolaireeah*
post office	**la oficina de correos** *lah ofeetheenah day korrayos*
shoe store	**la zapatería** *lah thapataireeah*
dry-cleaner	**la tintorería** *lah teentoraireeah*
grocery	**el ultramarinos** *el ooltramareenos*

❸ tobacconist

❻ bookstore

❾ bank

4 Useful phrases (3 minutes)

Familiarize yourself with these phrases.

Where is the hairdresser?	**¿Dónde está la peluquería?** *donday estah lah pelookaireeah*
Where do I pay?	**¿Dónde se paga?** *donday say pagah*
I'm just looking, thank you.	**Sólo estoy mirando, gracias.** *soloh estoy meerandoh grathyas*
Do you sell SIM cards?	**¿Tiene tarjetas SIM?** *tyenay tarhetas seem*
May I have two of those?	**¿Me pone dos de éstos?** *may ponay dos day estos*
Can I place an order?	**¿Puedo hacer un pedido?** *pwedoh ahther oon pedeedoh*

5 Say it (2 minutes)

Where is the bank?

Do you sell cheese?

Where do I pay?

1 Warm up (1 minute)

What is Spanish for "40," "56," "77," "82," and "94"? (pp.10-11 and pp.30-1)

Say "I'd like a big room." (pp.64-5)

Ask "Do you have a small car?" (pp.64-5)

EN EL MERCADO
At the market

Spain uses the metric system of weights and measures, so you will need to ask for produce in kilograms or grams. Some larger items, such as melons or pineapples, tend to be sold by **la pieza** (as single items); other items, such as lettuce, may be sold in twos or threes.

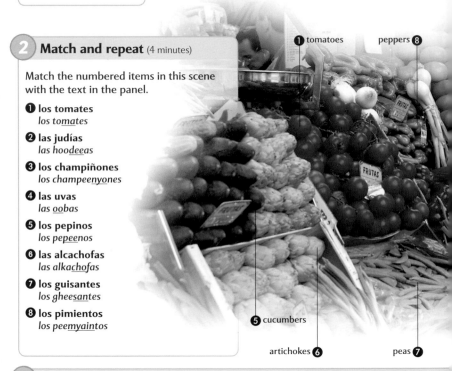

2 Match and repeat (4 minutes)

Match the numbered items in this scene with the text in the panel.

❶ **los tomates**
los tomates

❷ **las judías**
las hoodeeas

❸ **los champiñones**
los champeenyones

❹ **las uvas**
las oobas

❺ **los pepinos**
los pepeenos

❻ **las alcachofas**
las alkachofas

❼ **los guisantes**
los gheesantes

❽ **los pimientos**
los peemyaintos

❶ tomatoes   peppers ❽

❺ cucumbers

artichokes ❻   peas ❼

3 In conversation: (3 minutes)

Quisiera tomates.
keesyairah tomates

I'd like some tomatoes.

¿De los grandes o de los pequeños?
day los grandes oh day los pekenyos

The large ones or the small ones?

Dos kilos de los pequeños, por favor.
dos keelos day los pekenyos, por fabor

Two kilos of the small ones, please.

Cultural tip Spain uses the common European currency, the euro, which is divided into 100 **centimos**. Spanish-speaking countries in Central and South America all have their own currencies. Argentina, Chile, Uruguay, Colombia, and Mexico all call their currency the **peso**, which is divided into 100 **centavos**.

grapes **4**

mushrooms **3**

beans **2**

4 Useful phrases (5 minutes)

Learn these phrases. Then cover up the answers on the right. Read the English under the pictures and say the phrase in Spanish as shown on the right.

That sausage is too expensive.

Esa salchicha es demasiado cara.
ehsah salcheechah es demasyahdoh karah

How much is that one?

¿A cuánto está esa?
ah kwantoh estah ehsa

5 Say it (2 minutes)

Two kilos of peas, please.

The mushrooms are too expensive.

How much are the grapes?

That's all.

Eso es todo.
ehsoh es todoh

¿Algo más, señorita?
algoh mas, senyoreetah

Anything else, miss?

**Eso es todo, gracias.
¿Cuánto es?**
*ehsoh es todoh, grathyas.
kwantoh es*

That's all, thank you.
How much?

Tres cincuenta.
tres theenkwentah

Three-fifty.

EN EL SUPERMERCADO
At the supermarket

1 Warm up (1 minute)

What are these items you could buy in a supermarket? (pp.24-5)

la carne
el pescado
el queso
el zumo
el vino
el agua

Prices in supermarkets are usually lower than in smaller shops. They offer all kinds of products, with larger out-of-town **hipermercados** carrying clothes, household goods, lawn furniture, and home improvement products.

2 Match and repeat (5 minutes)

Look at the numbered product categories and match them to the Spanish words in the panel on the left.

❶ **los productos del hogar**
   los prodooktos del ohgar

❷ **la fruta**
   lah frootah

❸ **las bebidas**
   las bebeedas

❹ **los platos preparados**
   los platos preparados

❺ **los productos de belleza**
   los prodooktos day beyethah

❻ **los productos lácteos**
   los prodooktos lakteh-os

❼ **la verdura**
   lah berdoorah

❽ **los congelados**
   los konhelados

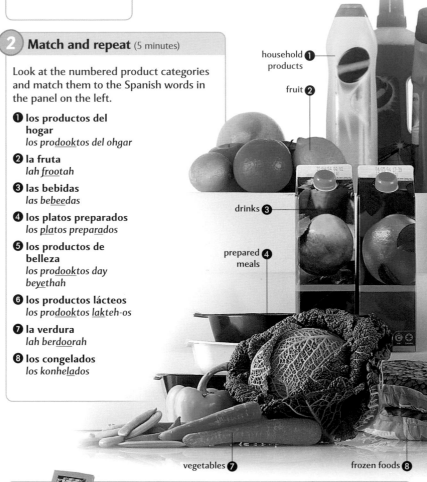

household ❶ products
fruit ❷
drinks ❸
prepared ❹ meals
vegetables ❼
frozen foods ❽

Cultural tip It is not usually possible to take unweighed fruit and vegetables sold by the kilo directly to the supermarket checkout. There is usually a separate counter or a self-service weighing machine.

3 Useful phrases (3 minutes)

Learn these phrases and then test yourself using the cover flap.

May I have a bag, please?	**¿Me da una bolsa, por favor?** *may dah oonah bolsah, por fabor*
Where are the drinks?	**¿Dónde están las bebidas?** *donday estan las bebeedas*
Where is the check-out, please?	**¿Dónde está la caja, por favor?** *donday estah lah kahah, por fabor*
Please type in your PIN.	**Por favor, meta su PIN.** *por fabor, metah soo peen*

❺ beauty products

❻ dairy products

4 Words to remember (4 minutes)

Learn these words and then test yourself using the cover flap.

bread	**el pan** *el pan*
milk	**la leche** *lah lechay*
butter	**la mantequilla** *lah mantekeeyah*
ham	**el jamón** *el hamon*
salt	**la sal** *lah sal*
pepper	**la pimienta** *lah peemyaintah*
laundry detergent	**el jabón de lavadora** *el habon day labadorah*
toilet paper	**el papel higiénico** *el papel eehyaineekoh*
diapers	**los pañales** *los panyales*

5 Say it (2 minutes)

Where are the dairy products?

May I have some cheese, please?

Where are the frozen foods?

LA ROPA Y LOS ZAPATOS
Clothes and shoes

1 Warm up (1 minute)

Say "I'd like...". (pp.22-3)

Ask "Do you have...?" (pp.14-15)

Say "38," "42," and "46." (pp.10-11 and pp.30-1)

Say "big," "small," "bigger," and "smaller." (pp.64-5)

Clothes and shoes are measured in metric sizes from 36 upward. Even allowing for conversion of sizes, Spanish clothes tend to be cut smaller than American ones. Clothes size is **la talla** but shoe size is **el número**.

2 Match and repeat (3 minutes)

Match the numbered items of clothing to the Spanish words in the panel on the left. Test yourself using the cover flap.

1 **la camisa**
   lah kameesah

2 **la corbata**
   lah korbatah

3 **la chaqueta**
   lah chaketah

4 **el bolsillo**
   el bolseeyoh

5 **la manga**
   lah mangah

6 **el pantalón**
   el pantalon

7 **la falda**
   lah faldah

8 **las medias**
   las medyas

9 **los zapatos**
   los thapatos

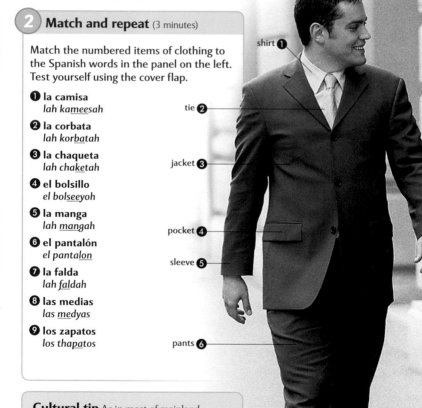

shirt **1**

tie **2**

jacket **3**

pocket **4**

sleeve **5**

pants **6**

Cultural tip As in most of mainland Europe, Spain uses the continental system of sizes. Women's clothes sizes usually range from 36 (US 6) through to 46 (US 18), and shoe sizes from 37 (US 5½) to 45 (US 12). For men's shirts, a size 41 is a 16-inch collar, 43 is a 17-inch collar, and 45 is an 18-inch collar.

3 Useful phrases (5 minutes)

Practice these phrases and then test yourself using the cover flap.

Do you have a larger size?	**¿Tiene una talla más grande?** _tyenay oonah tayah mas granday_
It's not what I want.	**No es lo que quiero.** _noh es loh kay kyairoh_
I'll take the pink one.	**Me quedo con el rosa.** _may kedoh kon el rrosah_

4 Words to remember (4 minutes)

Colors are adjectives (pp.64–5) and in most cases have a masculine and a feminine form. The feminine is usually formed by substituting an **a** for the final **o**.

red	**rojo/roja** _rrohoh/rrohah_
white	**blanco/blanca** _blankoh/blankah_
blue	**azul** _athool_
yellow	**amarillo/amarilla** _amareeyoh/amareeyah_
green	**verde** _berday_
black	**negro/negra** _negroh/negrah_

⑦ skirt

⑧ pantyhose

⑨ shoes

5 Say it (2 minutes)

What shoe size?

Do you have a black jacket?

Do you have a size 38?

Do you have a smaller size?

Respuestas
Answers (Cover with flap)

REPASE Y REPITA
Review and repeat

1 Market

❶ las alcachofas
las alkachofas

❷ los tomates
los tomates

❸ los guisantes
los gheesantes

❹ los pimientos
los peemyaintos

❺ las judías
las hoodeeas

1 Market (3 minutes)

Name the numbered vegetables in Spanish.

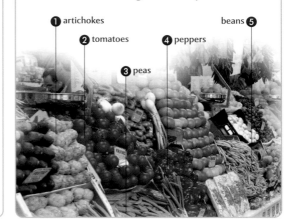

❶ artichokes
❷ tomatoes
❸ peas
❹ peppers
❺ beans

2 Description

❶ The shoes are too expensive.
❷ My room is very small.
❸ I need a softer bed.

2 Description (2 minutes)

What do these sentences mean?

❶ Los zapatos son demasiados caros.
❷ Mi habitación es muy pequeña.
❸ Necesito una cama más blanda.

3 Shops

❶ la panadería
lah panadaireeah

❷ la joyería
lah hoyehreeah

❸ la librería
lah leebraireeah

❹ la pescadería
lah peskadaireeah

❺ la pastelería
lah pastaylaireeah

❻ la carnicería
lah karneethaireeah

3 Shops (3 minutes)

Name the numbered shops in Spanish. Then check your answers.

❶ bread shop
❷ jeweler
❸ bookstore
❹ fishmonger
❺ bakery
❻ butcher

4 Supermarket (3 minutes)

What is the Spanish for the numbered product categories?

1 household products

2 beauty products

3 drinks

4 dairy products

5 vegetables

4 Supermarket

1 los productos del hogar
los prodooktos del ohgar

2 los productos de belleza
los prodooktos day beyethah

3 las bebidas
las bebeedas

4 los productos lácteos
los prodooktos lakteh-os

5 los congelados
los konhelados

5 Museum (4 minutes)

Follow this conversation, replying in Spanish following the English prompts.

Buenos días. ¿Qué desean?
1 I'd like five tickets.

Son setenta y cinco euros.
2 That's very expensive!

No hacemos descuentos a los niños.
3 How much is a guide?

Quince euros.
4 Good. And five tickets, please.

Noventa euros, por favor.
5 Here you are. Where are the restrooms?

A la derecha.
6 Thank you very much.

5 Museum

1 Quisiera cinco entradas.
keesyairah theenkoh entradas

2 ¡Es muy caro!
es mwee karoh

3 ¿Cuánto cuesta una guía?
kwantoh kwestah oonah gheeah

4 Bien. Y cinco entradas, por favor.
Byen. ee theenkoh entradas, por fabor

5 Aquí tiene. ¿Dónde están los servicios?
ahkee tyenay. donday estan los serbeethyos

6 Muchas gracias.
moochas grathyas

LAS OCUPACIONES
Jobs

Say "from which platform?" (pp.38–9)

What is the Spanish for the following family members: sister, brother, mother, father, son, and daughter? (pp.10–11)

Some occupations have commonly used feminine alternatives—for example, **enfermero** (*male nurse*) and **enfermera** (*female nurse*). Others remain the same. When you describe your occupation, you don't use **un/una** (*a*), saying simply **soy abogado** (*I'm a lawyer*), for example.

2 Words to remember: jobs (7 minutes)

Familiarize yourself with these words and test yourself using the flap. The feminine alternative is shown in brackets.

médico *medeekoh*	doctor
dentista *denteestah*	dentist
enfermero/-a *enfermairoh/-ah*	nurse
profesor/-sora *profaysor/-sorah*	teacher
abogado/-a *abogadoh/-ah*	lawyer
contable *kontablay*	accountant
diseñador/-dora *deesenyador/-dorah*	designer
consultor/-a *konsooltor/-ah*	consultant
secretario/-a *sekraytareeoh(-ah)*	secretary
comerciante *komerthyantay*	shopkeeper
electricista *elektreetheestah*	electrician
fontanero/-a *fontanairoh/-ah*	plumber
cocinero/-a *kotheenairoh/-ah*	cook/chef
albañil *albanyeel*	handyman
autónomo/-a *aootohnomoh/-ah*	self-employed

Soy fontanero.
soy fontanairoh
I'm a plumber.

Es estudiante.
es estoodyantay
She is a student.

3 Put into practice (4 minutes)

Join in this conversation. Read the Spanish on the left and follow the instructions to make your reply. Then test yourself.

¿Cuál es su profesión?
kwal es soo profesyon

Soy consultor.
soy konsooltor

What do you do?

Say: I am a consultant.

¿Para qué empresa trabaja?
parah kay empresah trabahah

Soy autónomo.
soy aootohnomoh

What company do you work for?

Say: I'm self-employed.

¡Qué interesante!
kay intairaysantay

¿Y cuál es su profesión?
ee kwal es soo profesyon

How interesting!

Say: And what is your profession?

Soy dentista.
soy denteestah

I'm a dentist.

Say: My sister is a dentist, too.

Mi hermana es dentista también.
mee airrmanah es denteestah tambyen

4 Words to remember: workplace (3 minutes)

La oficina central está en Madrid.
lah ofeetheenah thentral estah en madreed
Headquarters is in Madrid.

Familiarize yourself with these words and test yourself.

branch	**la sucursal** *lah sookoorsal*
department	**el departamento** *el departamaintoh*
manager	**el jefe** *el hefay*
employee	**el empleado** *el emplay-ahdoh*
reception	**la recepción** *lah rrethepthyon*
trainee	**el aprendiz** *el ahprendeeth*

1 Warm up (1 minute)

Practice different ways of introducing yourself in different situations (pp. 8–9). Mention your name, occupation (pp.78–9), and any other information you'd like to volunteer.

LA OFICINA
The office

An office environment or business situation has its own vocabulary in any language, but there are many items that are virtually universal. Be aware that Spanish computer keyboards have a different layout from the standard "QWERTY" convention; they also include ñ, vowels with accents, ¡, and ¿.

2 Words to remember (5 minutes)

Familiarize yourself with these words. Read them aloud several times and try to memorize them. Conceal the Spanish with the cover flap and test yourself.

el monitor *el moneetor*	monitor
el ratón *el rraton*	mouse
el correo electrónico *el korrayoh elektroneekoh*	email
el internet *el eenternet*	internet
la contraseña *lah kontrasenyah*	password
la mensajería de voz *lah mensahereeah day both*	voicemail
la contraseña del wifi *lah kontrasenyah del weefee*	Wi-Fi code
la fotocopiadora *lah fotokopyadorah*	photocopier
la agenda *lah ah-hendah*	planner
la tarjeta de visita *lah tarhetah day beeseetah*	business card
la reunión *lah reh-oonyon*	meeting
la conferencia *lah konfairentheeah*	conference
el orden del día *el orden del deeah*	agenda

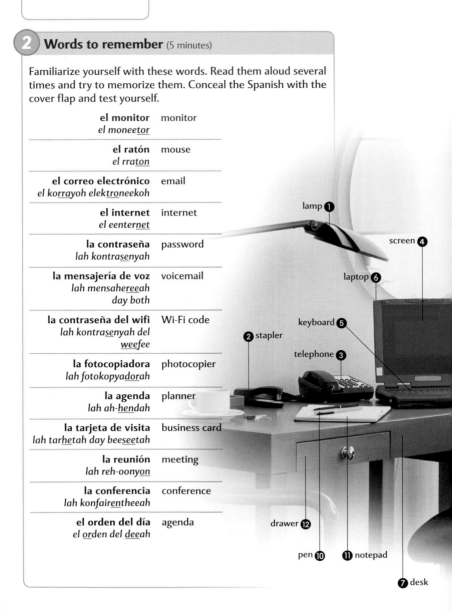

lamp ❶

screen ❹

laptop ❻

keyboard ❺

❷ stapler

telephone ❸

drawer ⓬

pen ❿   ⓫ notepad

❼ desk

3 Useful phrases (2 minutes)

Learn these phrases and then test yourself using the cover flap.

I need to make some photocopies.	**Necesito hacer unas fotocopias.** *netheseetoh ahther oonas fotokopyas*
I'd like to arrange an appointment.	**Quisiera organizar una cita.** *keesyairah organeethar oonah theetah*
I want to send an email.	**Quiero mandar un correo electrónico.** *kyairoh mandar oon korrayoh elektroneekoh*

4 Match and repeat (5 minutes)

Match the numbered items to the Spanish words on the left.

❶ **la lámpara**
lah lamparah

❷ **la grapadora**
lah grapadohrah

❸ **el teléfono**
el telefonoh

❹ **la pantalla**
lah pantayah

❺ **el teclado**
el tekladoh

❻ **el portátil**
el portateel

❼ **la mesa de escritorio**
lah mesah day eskreetoryoh

❽ **el reloj**
el rrelokh

❾ **la impresora**
lah impresorah

❿ **el bolígrafo**
el boleegrafoh

⓫ **el bloc**
el blok

⓬ **el cajón**
el kahon

⓭ **la silla giratoria**
lah seeyah heeratoreeah

5 Say it (2 minutes)

I'd like to arrange a conference.

I have a laptop.

Do you have email?

clock ❽

printer ❾

⓭ swivel chair

EL MUNDO ACADÉMICO
Academic world

1 Warm up (1 minute)

Say "library" and "How interesting!" (pp.48-9, pp.78-9)

Ask "What is your profession?" and answer "I'm a designer." (pp.78-9)

In Spain students are selected for a bachelor's degree (**una licenciatura**) by an average of secondary school grades and an exam. After graduation some students go on to **un máster** (master's degree) or **un doctorado** (PhD).

2 Useful phrases (3 minutes)

Practice these phrases and then test yourself using the cover flap.

¿Cuál es su especialidad? *kwal es soo espetheeahleedad*	What is your field?
Hago investigación en bioquímica. *ahgoh inbesteegathyon en beeohkeemeekah*	I am doing research in biochemistry.
Soy licenciado en derecho. *soy leethentheeahdoh en derechoh*	I have a degree in law.
Voy a dar una conferencia sobre arquitectura. *boy ah dar oonah konfairayntheeah sobray arkeetektoorah*	I'm going to give a lecture on architecture.

3 In conversation (5 minutes)

Hola, soy la profesora Fernández.
o-lah, soy lah profaysorah fernandeth

Hello, I'm Professor Fernandez.

¿De qué universidad es usted?
deh kay ooneeberseedad es oosted

What university are you from?

De la Universidad de Murcia.
deh lah ooneeberseedad deh moortheeah

From the University of Murcia.

4 Words to remember (4 minutes)

Familiarize yourself with these words and then test yourself.

Tenemos un stand en la feria.
tenemos oon estand en la fereeah
We have a stand at the trade fair.

conference/lecture	**la conferencia** *lah konfairaintheeah*
trade fair	**la feria** *lah fereeah*
seminar	**el seminario** *el semeenaryoh*
lecture hall	**el anfiteatro** *el anfeetay-ahtroh*
conference room	**la sala de conferencias** *lah sahlah deh konferaintheeas*
exhibition	**la exposición** *lah eksposeethyon*
library	**la biblioteca** *lah bibleeotekah*
assistant professor	**el profesor de universidad** *el profaysor deh ooneeberseedad*
professor	**el catedrático** *el katedrateekoh*
medicine	**medicina** *medeetheenah*
science	**ciencias** *thyaintheeas*
literature	**literatura** *leetairatoorah*
engineering	**ingeniería** *inhenyaireeah*

5 Say it (2 minutes)

I'm doing research in medicine.

I have a degree in literature.

She's the professor.

¿Cuál es su especialidad?
kwal es soo espethyaleedad

What's your field?

Hago investigación en ingeniería.
ahgoh inbesteegathyon en inhenyaireeah

I'm doing research in engineering.

¡Qué interesante! Yo también.
keh intairaysantay. yoh tambeeayn

How interesting! I am, too.

1 Warm up (1 minute)

Ask "Can I ...?" (pp.34-5)

Say "I want to send an email." (pp.80-1)

Say "I'd like to arrange an appointment." (pp.80-1)

LOS NEGOCIOS
In business

You will receive a more friendly reception and make a good impression if you make the effort to begin a meeting with a short introduction in Spanish, even if your vocabulary is limited. After that, all parties will probably be happy to continue the proceedings in English.

2 Words to remember (6 minutes)

Familiarize yourself with these words and then test yourself by covering the Spanish with the cover flap.

el cliente
el klyaintay
client

el programa *el programah*	schedule
la entrega *lah entraygah*	delivery
el pago *el pahgoh*	payment
el presupuesto *el praysoopwestoh*	budget/ estimate
el precio *el praythyoh*	price
el documento *el dokoomentoh*	document
la factura *lah faktoorah*	invoice
la propuesta *lah propwestah*	proposal
los beneficios *los baynayfeethyos*	profits
las ventas *las bentas*	sales
los números *los noomeros*	figures

el informe
el informay
report

Cultural tip A long lunch with wine is still a regular feature of doing business in Spain. As a visiting client you can expect to be taken out to a restaurant, and as a supplier you should consider entertaining your business customers.

3 Useful phrases (6 minutes)

Practice these useful business phrases and then test yourself using the cover flap.

¿Firmamos el contrato?
feermamos el kontratoh
Shall we sign the contract?

el ejecutivo
el eh-hekooteeboh
executive

el contrato
el kontratoh
contract

Me manda el contrato, por favor.
may mandah el kontratoh, por fabor

Please send me the contract.

¿Hemos acordado un programa?
ehmos akordadoh oon programah

Have we agreed a schedule?

¿Cuándo puede hacer la entrega?
kwandoh pweday ahther lah entregah

When can you make the delivery?

¿Cuál es el presupuesto?
kwal es el praysoopwestoh

What's the budget?

¿Me puede mandar la factura?
may pweday mandar lah faktoorah

Can you send me the invoice?

4 Say it (2 minutes)

Can you send me the estimate?

Have we agreed on a price?

What are the profits?

REPASE Y REPITA
Review and repeat

1 At the office

❶ **la grapadora**
lah grapadorah

❷ **la lámpara**
lah lamparah

❸ **el portátil**
el portateel

❹ **el bolígrafo**
el boleegrafoh

❺ **el reloj**
el rrelokh

❻ **el bloc**
el blok

❼ **la mesa de escritorio**
lah mesah day eskreetoryoh

1 At the office (4 minutes)

Name these items.

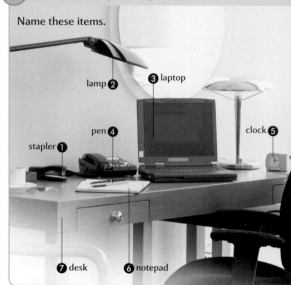

lamp ❷

❸ laptop

pen ❹

clock ❺

stapler ❶

❼ desk   ❻ notepad

2 Jobs

❶ **médico**
medeekoh

❷ **fontanero/-a**
fontanairoh/-ah

❸ **comerciante**
komerthyantay

❹ **contable**
kontablay

❺ **estudiante**
estoodyantay

❻ **abogado/-a**
abogadoh/-ah

2 Jobs (3 minutes)

What are these jobs in Spanish?

❶ doctor

❷ plumber

❸ shopkeeper

❹ accountant

❺ student

❻ lawyer

3 Work (4 minutes)

Answer these questions
following the English prompts.

¿Para qué empresa trabaja?
❶ Say: I am self-employed.

¿En qué universidad está?
❷ Say: I'm at the University
of Salamanca.

¿Cuál es su especialidad?
❸ Say: I'm doing research
in medicine.

¿Hemos acordado un programa?
❹ Say: Yes, my secretary has
the schedule.

3 Work

❶ **Soy autónomo.**
soy aootonomoh

❷ **Estoy en la
Universidad de
Salamanca.**
*estoy en lah
ooneeberseedad day
salamankah*

❸ **Hago investigación
en medicina.**
*ahgoh inbesteegathyon
en medeetheenah*

❹ **Sí. mi secretaria
tiene el programa.**
*see. mee sekretareeah
tyenay el programah*

4 How much? (4 minutes)

Answer the question with the amount shown
in brackets.

❶ **¿Cuánto cuesta el
desayuno?** (€3.50)

❷ **¿Cuánto cuesta la
habitación?** (€47)

❸ **¿Cuánto cuesta un
kilo de tomates?**
(€3.25)

❹ **¿Cuánto cuesta un
plaza para cuatro
noches?** (€60)

4 How much?

❶ **Son tres euros
cincuenta.**
*son tres eh-ooros
theenkwentah*

❷ **Son cuarenta y
siete euros.**
*son kwarentah ee
seeaytay eh-ooros*

❸ **Son tres euros
veinticinco.**
*son tres eh-ooros
beynteetheenkoh*

❹ **Son sesenta euros.**
son sesentah eh-ooros

1 Warm up (1 minute)

Say "I'm allergic to nuts."
(pp.24-5)

Say the verb "tener" (to
have) in all its forms: yo,
tú, él/ella, nosotros(-as),
vosotros(-as), ellos
(-as). (pp.14-15)

EN LA FARMACIA
At the pharmacy

Spanish pharmacists are qualified to give advice
and sell over-the-counter medicines, as well as
dispensing prescription medicines. There is
generally a **farmacia de guardia** (*duty
pharmacy*) to provide 24-hour service in every
town—a list is displayed in every pharmacy.

2 Match and repeat (3 minutes)

Match the numbered items to the Spanish
words in the panel on the left and test
yourself using the cover flap.

❶ **la venda**
lah bendah

❷ **el jarabe**
el harabay

❸ **las gotas**
las gotas

❹ **la tirita**
lah teereetah

❺ **la jeringuilla**
lah hereengheeyah

❻ **la crema**
lah kremah

❼ **el supositorio**
el sooposeetoryoh

❽ **la pastilla**
lah pasteeyah

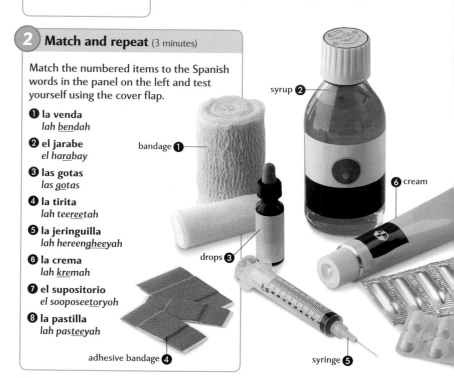

syrup ❷

bandage ❶

drops ❸

❻ cream

adhesive bandage ❹

syringe ❺

3 In conversation (3 minutes)

**Buenos días, señor.
¿Qué desea?**
*bwenos deeyas, senyor.
kay desayah*

Good morning, sir. What
would you like?

Tengo dolor de estómago.
tengoh dolor day estomagoh

I have a stomachache.

¿Tiene diarrea?
tyenay deeahrrayah

Do you have diarrhea?

4 **Words to remember** (2 minutes)

Familiarize yourself with these words and test yourself using the cover flap.

Tengo dolor de cabeza.
tengoh dolor day kabethah

I have a headache.

headache	**el dolor de cabeza** *el dolor day kabethah*
stomachache	**el dolor de estómago** *el dolor day estomagoh*
diarrhoea	**la diarrea** *lah deeahrrayah*
cold	**el resfriado** *el resfreeuhdoh*
cough	**la tos** *lah tos*
sunburn	**la insolación** *lah eensolatheeyon*
toothache	**el dolor de muelas** *el dolor day mwelas*

6 **Say it** (2 minutes)

I have a cold.

Do you have that as a cream?

He has a toothache.

7 suppository

8 tablet

5 **Useful phrases** (4 minutes)

Practice these phrases and then test yourself using the cover flap.

I have a sunburn.	**Tengo una insolación.** *tengoh oonah eensolatheeyon*
Do you have that as a syrup?	**¿Lo tiene en jarabe?** *loh tyenay en harabay*
I'm allergic to penicillin.	**Soy alérgico a la penicilina.** *soy alerheekoh ah lah peneetheeleenah*

No, pero tengo dolor de cabeza.
noh, peroh tengoh dolor day kabethah

No, but I have a headache.

Aquí tiene.
ahkee tyenay

Here you are.

¿Lo tiene en pastilla?
loh tyenay en pasteeyah

Do you have this as pills?

EL CUERPO
The body

1 **Warm up** (1 minute)

Say "I have a toothache" and "I have a sunburn." (pp.88-9)

Say the Spanish for "red," "green," "black," and "yellow." (pp.74-5)

You are most likely to need to refer to parts of the body in the context of illness—for example, when describing aches and pains to a doctor. The most common phrases for talking about discomfort are **Tengo un dolor en la/el...** (*I have a pain in the...*) and **Me duele la/el...** (*My ... hurts me*).

2 **Match and repeat: body** (6 minutes)

Match the numbered parts of the body with the list on the left. Test yourself by using the cover flap.

1 **la mano**
lah manoh

2 **la cabeza**
lah kabethah

3 **el hombro**
el ombroh

4 **el codo**
el kodoh

5 **el pelo**
el peloh

6 **el brazo**
el brathoh

7 **el cuello**
el kweyoh

8 **el pecho**
el pechoh

9 **el estómago**
el estomagoh

10 **la pierna**
lah pyairnah

11 **la rodilla**
lah rrodeeyah

12 **el pie**
el pee-ay

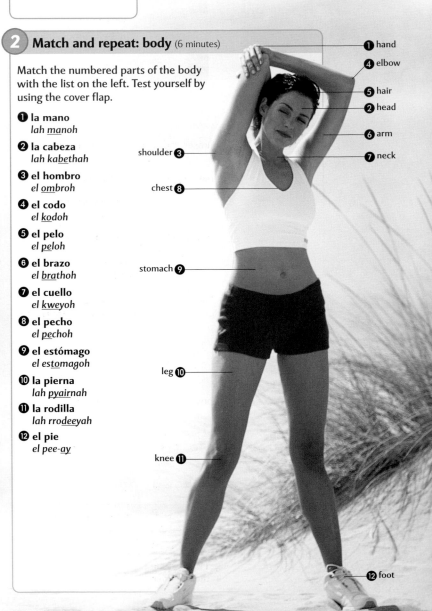

1 hand
4 elbow
5 hair
2 head
6 arm
shoulder **3**
7 neck
chest **8**
stomach **9**
leg **10**
knee **11**
12 foot

3 **Match and repeat: face** (3 minutes)

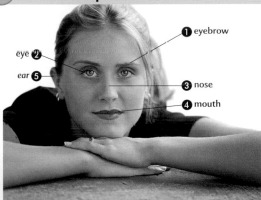

Match the numbered facial features with the list on the right.

1 eyebrow

eye **2**

ear **5**

3 nose

4 mouth

1 la ceja
lah thayah

2 el ojo
el oh-hoh

3 la nariz
lah nareeth

4 la boca
lah bokah

5 la oreja
lah ohrayah

4 **Useful phrases** (3 minutes)

Learn these phrases and then test yourself using the cover flap.

I have a pain in my back.	**Tengo un dolor en la espalda.** *tengoh oon dolor en lah espalda*
I have a rash on my arm.	**Tengo un sarpullido en el brazo.** *tengoh oon sarpooyeedoh en el brathoh*
I don't feel well.	**No me encuentro bien.** *noh may enkwentroh byen*

5 **Put into practice** (2 minutes)

Join in this conversation and test yourself using the cover flap.

¿Cuál es el problema?
kwal es el problemah

What's the problem?

Say: I don't feel well.

No me encuentro bien.
noh may enkwentroh byen

¿Dónde le duele?
donday lay dwelay

Where does it hurt?

Say: I have a pain in the shoulder.

Tengo un dolor en el hombro.
tengoh oon dolor en el ombroh

EN EL MÉDICO
At the doctor

1 **Warm up** (1 minute)

Say "I need some tablets." (pp.60-1, pp.88-9)

Say "He needs some cream." (pp.88-9)

What is the Spanish for "I don't have a son"? (pp.10-15)

Unless it's an emergency, you have to make an appointment with the doctor and pay when you leave. You may be able to reclaim the money if you have medical insurance. Your hotel, a local pharmacy, or a tourist information office may be able to tell you the names and addresses of local doctors.

2 **Useful phrases you may hear** (3 minutes)

Practice these phrases and then test yourself using the cover flap to conceal the Spanish on the left.

No es grave. *noh es gravay*	It's not serious.
Necesita hacerse unas pruebas. *netheseetah ahthersay oonas prwaybas*	You need to have some tests.
Tiene una infección de riñón. *tyenay oonah infekthyon day rreenyon*	You have a kidney infection.
Necesita ir al hospital. *netheseetah eer al ospeetal*	You need to go to hospital.

Le voy a dar una receta.
lay boy ah dar oonah rrethetah
I'm going to give you a prescription.

3 **In conversation** (5 minutes)

¿Cuál es el problema?
kwal es el problemah

What's the problem?

Tengo un dolor en el pecho.
tengoh oon dolor en el pechoh

I have a pain in my chest.

Déjeme que la examine.
dayhaymay kay lah eksameenay

Let me examine you.

4 Useful phrases you may need to say (4 minutes)

Estoy embarazada.
estoy embarathadah
I am pregnant.

Practice these phrases and then test yourself using the cover flap.

I am diabetic.	**Soy diabético/-a** *soy deeahbeteekoh/-ah*
I am epileptic.	**Soy epiléptico/-a.** *soy epeelepteekoh/-ah*
I have asthma.	**Soy asmático/-a.** *soy asmateekoh/-ah*
I have a heart condition.	**Tengo un problema de corazón.** *tengoh oon problemah day korathon*
I have a temperature.	**Tengo fiebre.** *tengoh fyaybray*
I feel faint.	**Estoy mareado.** *estoy maray-ahdoh*
It's urgent.	**Es urgente.** *es oorhentay*

Conversational tip

Before you go to Spain, find out if your health insurance covers emergency medical care in Europe; if it doesn't, purchase a travel medical insurance policy. For an ambulance, call 112.

5 Say it (2 minutes)

My son is diabetic.

I have a pain in my arm.

It's not urgent.

¿Es grave?
es gravay

Is it serious?

No, sólo tiene indigestión.
noh, soloh tyenay indeehestyon

No, you only have indigestion.

¡Menos mal!
maynos mal

What a relief!

EN EL HOSPITAL
At the hospital

1 Warm up (1 minute)

Say "How long is the trip?" (pp.42-3)

Ask "Is it serious?" (pp.92-3)

What is the Spanish for "mouth" and "head"? (pp.90-1)

It is useful to know a few basic phrases relating to hospitals and medical treatment for use in an emergency, or in case you need to visit a friend or colleague in the hospital. Most Spanish hospitals have only two beds per room with their own private bathroom facilities.

2 Useful phrases (5 minutes)

Familiarize yourself with these phrases. Conceal the Spanish with the cover flap and test yourself.

¿Cuáles son las horas de visita? _kwales son las oras day beeseetah_	What are the visiting hours?
¿Cuánto tiempo va a tardar? _kwantoh tyempoh bah ah tardar_	How long will it take?
¿Va a doler? _bah ah doler_	Will it hurt?
Túmbese aquí por favor. _toombesay ahkee por fabor_	Please lie down here.
No puede comer nada. _noh pweday komer nadah_	You cannot eat anything.
No mueva la cabeza. _noh mwebah lah kabethah_	Don't move your head.
Abra la boca por favor. _ahbrah lah bokah por fabor_	Please open your mouth.
Necesita un análisis de sangre. _netheseetah oon analeesees day sangray_	You need a blood test.

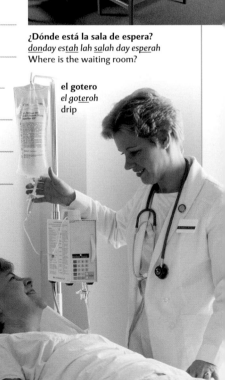

¿Dónde está la sala de espera?
donday estah lah salah day esperah
Where is the waiting room?

el gotero
el goteroh
drip

¿Se encuentra mejor?
say enkwentrah mehor
Are you feeling better?

3 Words to remember (4 minutes)

Su radiografía es normal.
soo rradyografeeah es normal
Your X-ray is normal.

Familiarize yourself with these words and test yourself using the cover flap.

emergency room	**el servicio de urgencias** *el serbeethyoh day oorhentheeas*
x-ray department	**el servicio de radiología** *el serbeethyoh day rradyoloheeah*
children's ward	**la sala de pediatría** *lah salah day pedeeatreeah*
operating room	**el quirófano** *el keerofanoh*
waiting room	**la sala de espera** *lah salah day esperah*
stairs	**las escaleras** *las eskaleras*

4 Put into practice (3 minutes)

Join in this conversation. Cover up the text on the right and complete the anwering part of the dialogue in Spanish. Check your answers and repeat if necessary.

Tiene una infección.
tyenay oonah infekthyon

You have an infection.

Ask: Do I need tests?

¿Necesito hacerme pruebas?
netheseetoh ahthermay prwaybas

Primero necesita un análisis de sangre.
preemeroh netheseetah oon analeesees day sangray

First you will need a blood test.

Ask: Will it hurt?

¿Me va a doler?
may bah ah doler

5 Say it (2 minutes)

Does he need a blood test?

Where is the children's ward?

Do I need an X-ray?

No, no se preocupe.
noh, noh say pray-okoopay

No. Don't worry.

Ask: How long will it take?

¿Cuánto tiempo va a tardar?
kwantoh tyempoh bah ah tardar

Respuestas
Answers (Cover with flap)

REPASE Y REPITA
Review and repeat

1 The body

❶ **la cabeza**
lah ka<u>beth</u>ah

❷ **el brazo**
el <u>brath</u>oh

❸ **el pecho**
el <u>pech</u>oh

❹ **el estómago**
el es<u>tom</u>agoh

❺ **la pierna**
lah <u>pyair</u>nah

❻ **la rodilla**
lah rro<u>deey</u>ah

❼ **el pie**
el pee-<u>ay</u>

1 The body (4 minutes)

Name the numbered body parts in Spanish.

❶ head
❷ arm
chest ❸
stomach ❹
leg ❺
knee ❻
❼ foot

2 On the phone

❶ **Quisiera hablar con Ana Flores.**
kees<u>yair</u>ah hab<u>lar</u> kon <u>a</u>nna <u>flor</u>es

❷ **Luis Cortés de Don Frío.**
looees kor<u>tes</u> day don <u>free</u>-oh

❸ **¿Puedo dejar un mens aje?**
<u>pwed</u>oh de<u>har</u> oon men<u>sah</u>ay

❹ **La cita el lunes a las once está bien.**
lah <u>theet</u>ah el <u>loon</u>es ah las <u>onth</u>ay es<u>tah</u> byen

❺ **Gracias, adiós.**
<u>grath</u>yas, addy-<u>os</u>

2 On the phone (4 minutes)

You are arranging an appointment. Follow the conversation, replying in Spanish following the English prompts.

Dígame, Apex Finanzas.
❶ I'd like to speak to Ana Flores

¿De parte de quién?
❷ Luis Cortés, of Don Frío.

Lo siento, está comunicando.
❸ Can I leave a message?

Sí, dígame.
❹ The appointment on Monday at 11am is fine.

Muy bien, adiós.
❺ Thank you, goodbye.

3 Clothing (3 minutes)

Say the Spanish words for the numbered items of clothing.

tie ❶

❷ jacket

❹ skirt

pants ❸

❻ pantyhose

shoes ❺

3 Clothing

❶ **la corbata**
lah korbatah

❷ **la chaqueta**
lah chaketah

❸ **el pantalón**
el pantalon

❹ **la falda**
lah faldah

❺ **los zapatos**
los thapatos

❻ **las medias**
las medeeas

4 At the doctor's (4 minutes)

Say these phrases in Spanish.

❶ I don't feel well.
❷ I have a heart condition.
❸ Do I need to go to hospital?
❹ I'm pregnant.

4 At the doctor's

❶ **No me encuentro bien.**
noh may enkwentroh byen

❷ **Tengo un problema de corazón.**
tengoh oon problemah day korathon

❸ **¿Necesito ir al hospital?**
netheseetoh eer al ospeetal

❹ **Estoy embarazada.**
estoy embarathadah

EN CASA
At home

Say the months of the year in Spanish. (pp.28-9)

Ask "Is there a parking lot?" and "Are there restrooms?" (pp.48-9 and pp.62-3)

Many city-dwellers live in apartment blocks (**edificios**), but in rural areas the houses tend to be single-family (**chalet**). If you want to know how big it is, you will need to ask in square meters. If you want to know how many bedrooms there are, ask **¿Cuántos dormitorios hay?**.

2 **Match and repeat** (5 minutes)

Match the numbered items to the list and test yourself using the cover flap.

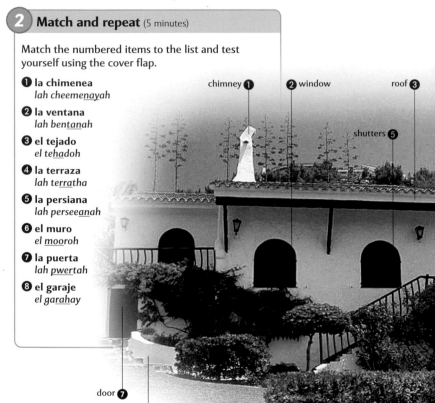

1 **la chimenea**
lah cheemenayah

2 **la ventana**
lah bentanah

3 **el tejado**
el tehadoh

4 **la terraza**
lah terratha

5 **la persiana**
lah perseeanah

6 **el muro**
el mooroh

7 **la puerta**
lah pwertah

8 **el garaje**
el garahay

chimney **1**   window **2**   roof **3**

shutters **5**

door **7**

wall **6**

Cultural tip You almost never see a Spanish home without shutters at every window. These are closed at night and often during the heat of the day in summer. Curtains, where they exist at all, tend to be more for decoration. Carpets are not popular in Spanish homes; ceramic tiles or parquet floors with rugs are a more common flooring solution.

3 Words to remember (4 minutes)

¿Cuánto es el alquiler al mes?
kwantoh es el alkeeler al mes
What is the rent per month?

Familiarize yourself with these words and test yourself using the cover flap.

room	**la habitación** *lah abeetathyon*
floor	**el suelo** *el sweloh*
ceiling	**el techo** *el techoh*
bedroom	**el dormitorio** *el dormeetoreeoh*
bathroom	**el cuarto de baño** *el kwartoh day banyoh*
kitchen	**la cocina** *lah kotheenah*
dining room	**el comedor** *el komedor*
living room	**el cuarto de estar** *el kwartoh day estar*
basement	**el sótano** *el sotahnoh*
attic	**el ático** *el ahteekoh*

terrace ❹

4 Useful phrases (3 minutes)

Practice these phrases and test yourself.

¿Hay un garaje?
ah-ee oon garahay

Is there a garage?

garage ❽

¿Cuándo está disponible?
kwandoh estah deesponeeblay

MAY MAI MAI MEI

When is it available?

5 Say it (2 minutes)

Is there a dining room?

Is it large?

Is it available in July?

¿Está amueblado?
estah amwebladoh

Is it furnished?

EN LA CASA
Inside the house

If you're renting a vacation house or villa in Spain, the most common option is to take it for a full month or, if not, for a **quincena**, the first or last fifteen days of the month. You will need to check in advance whether the cost of utilities is included in the rent. Most vacation homes have no telephone.

2 **Match and repeat** (3 minutes)

Match the numbered items to the list in the panel on the left. Then test yourself by concealing the Spanish with the cover flap.

1 **la encimera**
lah entheemerah

2 **el fregadero**
el fregaderoh

3 **el microondas**
el meekro-ondas

4 **el horno**
el ornoh

5 **la cocina**
lah kotheenah

6 **el frigorífico**
el freegoreefeekoh

7 **la mesa**
lah mesah

8 **la silla**
lah seeyah

5 stove **1** countertop

6 refrigerator

chair **8**

4 oven   table **7**

3 **In conversation** (3 minutes)

Este es el horno.
estay es el ornoh

This is the oven.

¿Hay también un lavavajillas?
ah-ee tambyen oon lababaheeyas

Is there a dishwasher as well?

Sí, y hay un congelador grande.
see, ee ah-ee oon konhelador granday

Yes, and there's a big freezer.

4 **Words to remember** (2 minutes)

Familiarize yourself with these words
and test yourself using the cover flap.

El sofá es nuevo.
el so<u>fah</u> es <u>nweboh</u>
The sofa is new.

wardrobe	**el armario** *el ar<u>mar</u>yoh*
sofa	**el sofá** *el so<u>fah</u>*
fireplace	**la chimenea** *lah cheeme<u>nay</u>ah*
carpet	**la moqueta** *luh mō<u>ke</u>tah*
bathtub	**la bañera** *lah ban<u>ye</u>rah*
toilet	**el váter** *el <u>ba</u>ter*
bathroom sink	**el lavabo** *el <u>la</u>baboh*

2 sink   microwave **3**

5 **Useful phrases** (4 minutes)

Practice these phrases and then test yourself.

The stove is broken.	**La cocina no funciona.** *lah ko<u>thee</u>nah* *noh foonthyo<u>nah</u>*
I don't like the curtains.	**No me gustan las cortinas.** *noh may <u>goos</u>tan* *las kor<u>tee</u>nas*
Is electricity included?	**¿Está incluida la electricidad?** *es<u>tah</u> eenkloo<u>ee</u>dah* *lah ehektreethee<u>dad</u>*

6 **Say it** (2 minutes)

Is there a microwave?

I like the fireplace.

What a soft sofa!

Todo está muy nuevo.
<u>to</u>doh es<u>tah</u> mwee <u>nweboh</u>

Everything is very new.

Y aquí está la lavadora.
ee ah<u>kee</u> es<u>tah</u> lah laba<u>do</u>rah

And here's the
washing machine.

¡Qué azulejos más bonitos!
kay ah-thoo<u>lay</u>hos mas bo<u>nee</u>tos

What beautiful tiles!

EL JARDÍN
The backyard

1 **Warm up** (1 minute)

Say "I need" and "you need." (pp.64-5, pp.92-4)

What is the Spanish for "day" and "month"? (pp.28-9)

Say the days of the week. (pp.28-9)

The yard of a house or villa may be communal, or at least partly shared. Check with the realtor or rental agent carefully to find out. In some cases, a charge for maintenance of the yard may be included with the rent of an apartment or house. Check such details with the agent.

2 **Words to remember** (3 minutes)

Familiarize yourself with these words and test yourself using the cover flap.

la máquina cortacésped *lah makeenah kortathesped*	lawnmower
la horca *lah orkah*	fork
la pala *lah palah*	spade
el rastrillo *el rrastreeyoh*	rake
el vivero *el beeberoh*	garden center

terrace **1**

tree **2**

flowers **7**

soil **3**

8 weeds

path **9**

3 Useful phrases (4 minutes)

Practice these phrases and then test yourself using the cover flap.

The gardener comes once a week.	**El jardinero viene una vez a la semana.** *el hardeenairoh byainay oonah beth ah lah semanah*
Can you mow the lawn?	**¿Puede cortar el césped?** *pweday kortar el thesped*
Is the yard private?	**¿Es el jardín privado?** *es el hardeen preebadoh*
The yard needs watering.	**El jardín necesita que lo rieguen.** *el hardeen netheseetah kay loh rreeayghen*

5 hedge
4 lawn
6 plants
10 flowerbed

4 Match and repeat (5 minutes)

Match the numbered items to the words in the panel on the right.

1 la terraza
lah terrathah

2 el árbol
el arbol

3 la tierra
lah tyairrah

4 el césped
el thesped

5 el seto
el setoh

6 las plantas
las plantas

7 las flores
las flores

8 las malas hierbas
las malas yerbas

9 el camino
el kameenoh

10 el parterre
el partairray

5 Say it (2 minutes)

The lawn needs water.

Are there any trees?

The gardener comes on Fridays.

LOS ANIMALES DE COMPAÑÍA
Pets

Many Spanish families have pets—dogs are especially popular—and veterinary services are generally good. Ask your vet about the necessary paperwork if you are considering traveling to Spain with your pet.

1 **Warm up** (1 minute)

Say "My name is …".
(pp.8-9)

Say "Don't worry."
(pp.94-5)

What is "your" in Spanish? (pp.12-13)

2 **Match and repeat** (3 minutes)

Match the numbered animals to the Spanish words in the panel on the left. Then test yourself using the cover flap.

❶ el gato
el gatoh

❷ el conejo
el konehoh

❸ el pájaro
el paharoh

❹ el pez
el peth

❺ el perro
el perroh

❻ el hámster
el hamster

bird ❸

❷ rabbit

dog ❺

❶ cat

3 **Useful phrases** (4 minutes)

Learn these phrases and then test yourself using the cover flap.

¿Es bueno el perro? *es bwenoh el perroh*	Is this dog friendly?
¿Puedo llevar el perro? *pwedoh yebar el perroh*	Can I bring my dog?
Me dan miedo los gatos. *may dan myaydoh los gatos*	I'm afraid of cats.
Mi perro no muerde. *mee perroh noh mweday*	My dog doesn't bite.

Este gato está lleno de pulgas.
estay gatoh estah yenoh day poolgas
This cat is full of fleas.

Cultural tip Many dogs in Spain are working or guard dogs, and you may encounter them tethered or roaming free. Approach farms and rural houses with particular care. Look out for warning notices such as **¡Cuidado con el perro!** (*Beware of the dog*).

¡CUIDADO CON EL PERRU!

Mi perro no está bien.
mee perroh noh estah byen
My dog is not well.

6 hamster

fish **4**

4 Words to remember (4 minutes)

Familiarize yourself with these words and test yourself using the cover flap.

basket	**la cesta** *lah thestah*
cage	**la jaula** *lah haoolah*
bowl	**el bol** *el bol*
collar	**el collar** *el koyar*
lead	**la correa** *lah korray-ah*
vet	**el veterinario** *el betereenaryoh*
vaccination	**la vacuna** *lah bakoonah*
pet passport	**el pasaporte de animales** *el pasaportay* *day aneemales*
flea spray	**el spray antipulgas** *el espraee anteepoolgas*

5 Put into practice (3 minutes)

Join in this conversation. Read the Spanish on the left and follow the instructions to make your reply. Then test yourself by concealing the answers with the cover flap.

¿Es suyo este perro?
es sooyoh estay perroh

Is this your dog?

Say: Yes, his name is Sandy.

Sí, se llama Sandy.
see, say yamah Sandy

Me dan miedo los perros.
may dan myaydoh los perros

I'm afraid of dogs.

Say: Don't worry.
He's friendly.

No se preocupe.
Es bueno.
noh say prayohkoopay.
es bwenoh

REPASE Y REPITA
Review and repeat

Respuestas
Answers (Cover with flap)

1 Colors

❶ negra
negrah

❷ pequeños
pekenyos

❸ rojo
rrohoh

❹ verde
berday

❺ amarillos
amareeyos

1 Colors (4 minutes)

Complete the sentences with the Spanish word for the color in brackets. Watch out for masculine and feminine.

❶ Quisiera la camisa _____. (black)

❷ Estos zapatos son muy _____. (small)

❸ ¿Tiene este traje en _____? (red)

❹ No, pero lo tengo en _____. (green)

❺ Quiero los zapatos _____. (yellow)

2 Kitchen

❶ la cocina
lah kotheenah

❷ el frigorífico
el freegoreefeekoh

❸ el fregadero
el fregaderoh

❹ el microondas
el meekro-ondas

❺ el horno
el ornoh

❻ la silla
lah seeyah

❼ la mesa
lah mesah

2 Kitchen (4 minutes)

Say the Spanish words for the numbered items.

stove ❶   refrigerator ❷

❺ oven   chair ❻

Respuestas
Answers (Cover with flap)

3 House (4 minutes)

You are visiting a house in Spain. Join in the conversation, asking questions in Spanish following the English prompts.

Éste es el cuarto de estar.
❶ What a lovely fireplace.

Sí, y tiene una cocina muy grande.
❷ How many bedrooms are there?

Hay tres dormitorios.
❸ Do you have a garage?

Sí, pero no hay un jardín.
❹ When is it available?

En julio.
❺ What is the rent a month?

3 House

❶ **¡Qué chimenea más bonita!**
kay cheemenayah mas boneetah

❷ **¿Cuántos dormitorios hay?**
kwantos dormeetoreeos ah-ee

❸ **¿Tiene garaje?**
tyenay garahay

❹ **¿Cuándo está disponible?**
kwandoh estah deesponeeblay

❺ **¿Cuánto es el alquiler al mes?**
kwantoh es el alkeeler al mes

4 At home (3 minutes)

Say the Spanish for the following items.

❶ washing machine
❷ sofa
❸ attic
❹ dining room
❺ tree
❻ garden

microwave ❹

❸ sink

table ❼

4 At home

❶ **la lavadora**
lah labadorah

❷ **el sofá**
el sofah

❸ **el ático**
el ahteekoh

❹ **el comedor**
el komedor

❺ **el árbol**
el arbol

❻ **el jardín**
el hardeen

Warm up (1 minute)

Ask "How do I get to the bank?" and "How do I get to the post office?" (pp.50-1)

What's the Spanish for "passport"? (pp.54-5)

How do you ask "What time is the meeting?" (pp.30-1)

EL BANCO Y LA OFICINA DE CORREOS
Bank and post office

Banks and post offices usually open only until lunchtime (approximately 2 pm) and are generally closed on weekends. **Cajas de ahorros** (*savings banks*) have different hours. In the summer, opening times may be shorter.

Words to remember: mail (3 minutes)

los sellos *los seyos*	stamps
la postal *lah postal*	postcard
el paquete *el paketay*	package
por avión *por abyon*	by air mail
el correo certificado *el korrayoh therteefeekadoh*	registered mail
el buzón *el boothon*	mailbox
el código postal *el kodeegoh postal*	postal (ZIP) code
el cartero *el kartairoh*	mail carrier

Familiarize yourself with these words and test yourself using the cover flap to conceal the Spanish on the left.

el sobre
el sobray
envelope

¿Cuánto es para el Reino Unido?
kwantoh es parah el rrayeenoh ooneedoh
How much is it to the United Kingdom?

In conversation (3 minutes)

Quisiera sacar dinero.
keesyairah sakar deeneroh

I'd like to withdraw some money.

¿Tiene identificación?
tyenay eedenteefeekathyon

Do you have any ID?

Sí, aquí tiene mi pasaporte.
see, ahkee tyenay mee pasaportay

Yes, here's my passport.

¿Cómo puedo pagar?
komoh pwedoh pagar
How can I pay?

4 Words to remember: bank (2 minutes)

Familiarize yourself with these words and test yourself using the cover flap to cover the Spanish on the right.

PIN	**el pin** *el peen*
bank	**el banco** *el bankoh*
teller	**el cajero** *el kaheroh*
ATM	**el cajero automático** *el kaheroh aootomateekoh*
notes (bills)	**los billetes** *los beeyetes*
credit card	**la tarjeta de crédito** *lah tarhetah day kredeetoh*

5 Useful phrases (4 minutes)

Practice these phrases and then test yourself using the cover flap.

I'd like to change some money.	**Quisiera cambiar dinero.** *keesyairah kambyar deeneroh*
What is the exchange rate?	**¿A cuánto está el cambio?** *ah kwantoh estah el kambyoh*
I'd like to withdraw some money.	**Quisiera sacar dinero.** *keesyairah sakar deeneroh*

6 Say it (2 minutes)

I'd like to pay by credit card.

Do I need my PIN?

How much is it for a postcard?

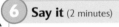

Meta su pin, por favor.
metah soo peen, por fabor

Please type in your PIN.

¿Tengo que firmar también?
tengoh kay feermar tambyen

Do I have to sign, too?

No, no hace falta.
noh, noh ahthay faltah

No, that's not necessary.

LOS SERVICIOS
Services

You can combine the Spanish words on these pages with the vocabulary you learned in week 10 to help you explain basic problems and cope with arranging most repairs. When negotiating building work or a repair, it's a good idea to agree on the price and method of payment in advance.

Warm up (1 minute)

What is the Spanish for "doesn't work"? (pp.60-1)

What's the Spanish for "today" and "tomorrow"? (pp.28-9)

Words to remember (4 minutes)

Familiarize yourself with these words and test yourself using the cover flap.

el fontanero *el fontanairoh*	plumber
el electricista *el ehlektreetheestah*	electrician
el mecánico *el mekaneekoh*	mechanic
el albañil *el albanyeel*	handyman
la asistenta *lah aseestentah*	cleaner
el pintor *el peentor*	decorator
el carpintero *el karpeenteroh*	carpenter
el técnico *el tekneekoh*	technician

la llave de tuercas
lah yabay day twerkas
tire iron

No necesito un mecánico.
noh netheseetoh oon mekaneekoh
I don't need a mechanic.

In conversation (3 minutes)

La lavadora no funciona.
lah labadorah noh foothyonah

The washing machine is not working.

Sí, la manguera está rota.
see, lah mangherah estah rrotah

Yes, the hose is broken.

¿La puede arreglar?
lah pweday arreglar

Can you repair it?

4 Useful phrases (3 minutes)

Practice these phrases and then test yourself using the cover flap.

Can you clean the bathroom?	**¿Puede limpiar el cuarto de baño?** _pweday leempyar el kwurtoh day banyoh_
Can you repair the boiler?	**¿Puede arreglar la caldera?** _pweday arreglar lah kalderah_
Do you know a good electrician?	**¿Conoce a un buen electricista?** _konothay ah oon bwen ehlektreetheestah_

¿Dónde me pueden arreglar la plancha?
donday may pweden arreglar lah planchah
Where can I get the iron repaired?

5 Put into practice (4 minutes)

Empiezo el trabajo mañana.
empyaythoh el trabahoh manyanah
I start the job tomorrow.

los planos
los planos
plans

Practice these phrases. Cover the text on the right and complete the dialogue in Spanish. Check your answers and repeat if necessary.

Su verja está rota.
soo berhah estah rrotah

Your gate is broken.

Ask: Do you know a good handyman?

¿Conoce a un buen albañil?
konothay ah oon bwen albanyeel

Sí, hay uno en el pueblo.
see, ah-ee oonoh en el pwebloh

Yes, there is one in the village.

Ask: Do you have his phone number?

¿Tiene su número de teléfono?
tyenay soo noomeroh day telefonoh

No, va a necesitar una nueva.
noh, bah ah netheseetar oonah nwebah

No, you'll need a new one.

¿Lo puede hacer hoy?
loh pweday ahther oy

Can you do it today?

No, volveré mañana.
noh, bolberay manyanah

No. I'll come back tomorrow.

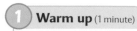

1 **Warm up** (1 minute)

Say the days of the week in Spanish. (pp.28-9)

How do you say "cleaner"? (pp.110-11)

Say "It's 9:30," "10:45," "12:00." (pp.30-1)

VENIR
To come

The verb **venir** (*to come*) is one of the most useful verbs. As well as the main verb (see below) it is worth knowing the command **¡ven!/¡venga!** (*come here!* informal/formal). Note that with me becomes **conmigo** and with you **contigo**: **ven conmigo** (*come with me*); **vengo contigo** (*I'm going with you*).

2 **Venir: to come** (6 minutes)

Say the different forms of the verb aloud, reading from the table. Use the cover flaps to test yourself and, when you are confident, practice the sample sentences listed below.

Vienen en muchos colores.
beeaynen en moochos kolores
They come in many colours.

yo vengo *yoh bengoh*	I come
tú vienes/usted viene *too byenes/oosted byenay*	you come (informal/formal singular)
él/ella viene *el/eh-yah byenay*	he/she comes
nosotros(-as) venimos *nosotros(-as) beneemos*	we come
vosotros(-as) venís *bosotros(-as) benees*	you come (informal plural)
ustedes vienen *oostedes byenen*	you come (formal plural)
ellos/ellas vienen *eh-yos/eh-yas byenen*	they come

Vengo ahora. *bengoh ah-orah*	I'm coming now.
Venimos todos los martes. *beneemos todos los martes*	We come every Tuesday.
Vienen en tren. *byenen en tren*	They come by train.

Conversational tip To say "*I come from the US*" in Spanish, you have to use the verb *to be*, as in "**soy estadounidense**" (*I am from the US*). When you use the verb *to come*, as in "**Vengo de Nueva York**," it means you have just arrived from New York.

3 Useful phrases (4 minutes)

Learn these phrases and then test yourself using the cover flap.

When can I come?	**¿Cuándo puedo venir?** _kwandoh pwedoh beneer_
Does it come in size 44?	**¿Viene en la talla 44?** _byenay en lah tayah kwarentah ee kwatroh_
The cleaner comes every Monday.	**La asistenta viene todos los lunes.** _lah aseestentah byenay todos los loones_
Come with me. (informal/formal)	**Ven conmigo/ Venga conmigo.** _ben konmeegoh/ bengah konmeegoh_

¿Puede venir el viernes?
pweday beneer el byairnes
Can you come on Friday?

4 Put into practice (4 minutes)

Practice these phrases. Then cover the text on the right and say the anwering part of the dialogue in Spanish. Check your answers and repeat if necessary.

Peluquería Cristina, dígame. _pelookereeah kristeenah, deegamay_	**Quisiera una cita.** _keesyairah oonah theetah_
Christine's hair salon. Can I help you?	
Say: I'd like an appointment.	

¿Cuándo quiere venir? _kwandoh kyairay beneer_	**Hoy, si es posible.** _oy, see es poseeblay_
When do you want to come?	
Say: Today, if possible.	

Sí, claro. ¿A qué hora? _see klaroh, ah kay orah_	**A las diez y media.** _ah las dyeth ee medeeah_
Yes of course. What time?	
Say: At 10.30.	

1 Warm up (1 minute)

What's the Spanish for "big" and "small"?
(pp.64-5)

Say "The room is big" and "The bed is small."
(pp.64-5)

LA POLICÍA Y EL DELITO
Police and crime

While in Spain, if you are the victim of a crime, you should go to the police station to report it, or in an emergency you can dial 112. You may have to explain your complaint in Spanish, so some basic vocabulary is useful.

2 Words to remember: crime (4 minutes)

Familiarize yourself with these words.

el robo *el rroboh*	robbery
la denuncia *lah denoontheeah*	police report
el ladrón *el ladron*	thief
la policía *lah poleetheeah*	police
la declaración *lah deklarathyon*	statement
el testigo *el testeegoh*	witness
el abogado *el abogadoh*	lawyer

Necesito un abogado.
netheseetoh oon abogadoh
I need a lawyer.

3 Useful phrases (3 minutes)

Learn these phrases and then test yourself.

Me han robado. *may an rrobadoh*	I've been robbed.
¿Qué han robado? *kay an rrobadoh*	What was stolen?
¿Vió quién lo hizo? *byoh kyain loh eethoh*	Did you see who did it?
¿Cuándo ocurrió? *kwandoh okoorryoh*	When did it happen?

la cámara de fotos
lah kamarah day fotos
camera

la cartera
la karterah
wallet

4 Words to remember: appearance (5 minutes)

Learn these words. Remember, some adjectives have a feminine form.

man	**el hombre** *el ombray*
woman	**la mujer** *lah moo-hair*
tall	**alto/alta** *altoh/altah*
short	**bajo/baja** *bahoh/bahah*
young	**joven** *hoben*
old	**viejo/vieja** *byayhoh/byayhah*
fat	**gordo/gorda** *gordoh/gordah*
thin	**delgado/delgada** *delgadoh/delgadah*
long/short hair	**el pelo largo/corto** *el peloh largoh/kortoh*
glasses	**las gafas** *las gafas*
beard	**la barba** *la barbah*

Él es bajo y tiene bigote.
el es bahoh ee tyenay beegotay
He is short and has a moustache.

Tiene el pelo negro y corto.
tyenay el peloh negroh ee kortoh
He has short, black hair.

Cultural tip In Spain there is a difference between **la guardia civil** and **la policía**. **La policía** are the local police while **la guardia civil** operates in airports and patrols the national road system. The police uniforms are blue and those of the **guardia civil** are green.

---

5 Put into practice (2 minutes)

Practice these phrases. Then cover the text on the right and follow the instructions to make your reply in Spanish.

¿Cómo era? **Bajo y gordo.**
komoh ehrah *bahoh ee gordoh*

What did he look like?

Say: Short and fat.

¿Y el pelo? **Largo y con barba.**
ee el peloh *largoh ee kon barbah*

And his hair?

Say: Long with a beard.

REPASE Y REPITA
Review and repeat

1 To come

❶ **vienen**
byenen

❷ **viene**
byenay

❸ **venimos**
beneemos

❹ **venís**
benees

❺ **vengo**
bengoh

1 To come (3 minutes)

Fill in the blanks with the correct form of **venir** (*to come*).

❶ Mis padres _____ a las cuatro.

❷ La asistenta _____ una vez a la semana.

❸ Nosotros _____ todos los martes.

❹ ¿ _____ vosotros con nosotros?

❺ Yo _____ en taxi.

2 Bank and post

❶ **los billetes**
los beeyetes

❷ **la postal**
lah postal

❸ **el paquete**
el paketay

❹ **el sobre**
el sobray

2 Bank and post (4 minutes)

Name these items.

❶ bills (notes)

postcard ❷

❸ package

envelope ❹

3 Appearance (4 minutes)

What do these descriptions mean?

❶ Es un hombre alto y delgado.

❷ Ella tiene el pelo corto y gafas.

❸ Soy baja y tengo el pelo largo.

❹ Ella es vieja y gorda.

❺ Él tiene los ojos azules y barba.

3 Appearance

❶ He's a tall, thin man.

❷ She has short hair and glasses.

❸ I'm short and I have long hair.

❹ She's old and fat.

❺ He has blue eyes and a beard.

4 The pharmacy (4 minutes)

You are asking a pharmacist for advice. Join in the conversation, replying in Spanish following the English prompts.

Buenos días, ¿qué desea?
❶ I have a cough.

¿Le duele el pecho?
❷ No, but I have a headache.

Tiene estas pastillas.
❸ Do you have that as a syrup?

Sí señor. Aquí tiene.
❹ Thank you. How much is that?

Cuatro euros.
❺ Here you are. Goodbye.

4 The pharmacy

❶ Tengo tos.
tengoh tos

❷ No, pero me duele la cabeza.
noh, peroh may dwelay lah kabethah

❸ ¿Lo tiene en jarabe?
loh tyenay en harabay

❹ Gracias. ¿Cuánto es?
grathyas. kwantoh es

❺ Aquí tiene. Adiós.
ahkee tyenay. addy-os

What is the Spanish for "museum" and "art gallery"? (pp.48–9)

Say "I don't like the curtains." (pp.100–1)

Ask "Do you want...?" informally. (pp.22–3)

EL OCIO
Leisure time

The Spanish pride themselves on their lively nightlife and support for the arts, including theatre and film. It is not unusual for Spaniards to number politics or philosophy among their interests. Be prepared for these topics to be the subject of conversation in social situations.

2 **Words to remember** (4 minutes)

Familiarize yourself with these words and test yourself using the cover flap to conceal the Spanish on the left.

el teatro _el te-ahtroh_	theater
el cine _el theenay_	cinema
la discoteca _lah deeskotekah_	discotheque
el deporte _el deportay_	sport
el turismo _el tooreesmoh_	sightseeing
la política _la poleeteekah_	politics
la música _lah mooseekah_	music
el arte _el artay_	art

Me encanta el baile.
me enkantah el baeelay
I love dancing.

3 **In conversation** (4 minutes)

Hola. ¿Quieres jugar al tenis hoy?
o-lah. kyaires hoogar al tenis oy

Hi, do you want to play tennis today?

No, no me gusta el deporte.
noh, noh may goostah el deportay

No, I don't like sport.

Y entonces, ¿qué te gusta?
ee entonthes, kay tay goostah

So then, what do you like?

los video-juegos
los beedayoh-hwegos
video games

la bailaora
lah baeelaorah
dancer

el traje típico
el trahay teepeekoh
traditional costume

4 Useful phrases (4 minutes)

Learn these phrases and then test yourself using the cover flap.

What are your (formal/ informal) interests?	**¿Cuáles son sus/ tus intereses?** *kwales son soos/ toos intereses*
I like the theater.	**Me gusta el teatro.** *may goostah el te-uhtroh*
I prefer the cinema.	**Yo prefiero el cine.** *yoh prefyairoh el theenay*
I'm interested in art.	**Me interesa el arte.** *may interesah el artay*
That bores me.	**Eso me aburre.** *ehsoh may aboorray*

5 Say it (2 minutes)

I'm interested in music.

I prefer sport.

I don't like video games.

Prefiero el turismo e ir de compras.
prefyairoh el tooreesmoh eh eer day kompras

I prefer sightseeing and shopping.

Eso a mí no me interesa.
ehsoh ah mee noh may interesah

That doesn't interest me.

No pasa nada. Me voy yo sola.
noh pasah nadah. may boy yoh solah

No problem. I'll go on my own.

1 Warm up (1 minute)

Ask "Do you (formal) want to play tennis?" (pp.118-19)

Say "I like the theater" and "I prefer sightseeing." (pp.118-19)

Say "That doesn't interest me." (pp.118-19)

EL DEPORTE Y LOS PASATIEMPOS
Sport and hobbies

Hacer (to do or to make) and **jugar** (to play) are the verbs used most when talking about sports and pastimes. **Jugar** is followed by **al** when you are talking about playing a sport, as in **juego al baloncesto** (I play basketball).

2 Words to remember (5 minutes)

Familiarize yourself with these words and then test yourself.

el fútbol/rugby el _footbol_/_roogbee_	soccer/rugby
el tenis/baloncesto el _tenis_/_balonthestoh_	tennis/ basketball
la natación lah nata_thyon_	swimming
la vela lah _belah_	sailing
la pesca lah _peskah_	fishing
la pintura lah peen_toorah_	painting
el ciclismo el thee_kleesmoh_	cycling
el senderismo el sende_reesmoh_	hiking

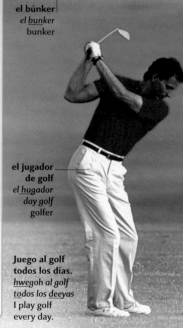

el búnker
el _bunker_
bunker

el jugador de golf
el _hugador_
day golf
golfer

Juego al golf todos los días.
hwegoh al golf todos los deeyas
I play golf every day.

3 Useful phrases (2 minutes)

Learn these phrases and then test yourself.

Juego al fútbol. _hwegoh al footbol_	I play soccer.
Juega al tenis. _hwegah al tenis_	He plays tennis.
Ella pinta. _eh-yah peentah_	She paints.

4 Hacer: to do or to make (4 minutes)

Hoy hace bueno.
oy ahthay bwenoh
It's nice (weather) today.

___ **la banderola**
lah bandairolah
flag

_____ **el campo de golf**
el kampoh day golf
golf course

Hacer is a useful verb meaning *to do* or *to make*. It is commonly used to describe leisure pursuits. **Hace** is also used to describe the weather.

I do	**yo hago** *yoh ahgoh*
you do (informal/ formal singular)	**tú haces/usted hace** *too ahthes/oosted ahthay*
he/she does	**él/ella hace** *el/eh-yah ahthay*
we do	**nosotros(-as) hacemos** *nosotros(-as) ahthemos*
you do (informal plural)	**vosotros(-as) hacéis** *bosotros(-as) ahthays*
you do (formal plural)	**ustedes hacen** *oostedes ahthen*
they do	**ellos/ellas hacen** *eh-yos/eh-yas ahthen*
What do you like doing? (informal/formal singular)	**¿Qué te/le gusta hacer?** *kay tay/lay goostah ahthair?*
I go hiking.	**Yo hago senderismo.** *yoh ahgoh sendereesmoh*

5 Put into practice (3 minutes)

Join in this conversation following the English prompts.

¿Qué te gusta hacer?
kay tay goostah ahthair

What do you like doing?

Say: I like playing tennis.

Me gusta jugar al tenis.
may goostah hoogar al tenis

¿Juegas al fútbol también?
hwegas al footbol tambyen

Do you play soccer, too?

Say: No, I play rugby.

No, juego al rugby.
noh, hwegoh al roogbee

¿Cuándo juegas?
kwandoh hwegas

When do you play?

Say: I play every week.

Juego todas las semanas.
hwegoh todas las semanas

Say "my husband" and "my wife." (pp.10-11)

Say the days of the week in Spanish. (pp.28-9)

Say "Sorry, I'm busy." (pp.32-3)

LA VIDA SOCIAL
Socializing

The Spanish dinner table is the center of the social world. You can expect to do a lot of your socializing around the table, enjoying food and wine. In general, it is best to use the more polite **usted** form to talk to older people and **tú** with the younger crowd.

2 **Useful phrases** (3 minutes)

Practice these phrases and then test yourself.

Me gustaría invitarte a cenar. *may goostareeah inbeetartay ah thenar*	I'd like to invite you to dinner.
¿Estás libre el miércoles que viene? *estas leebray el myairkoles kay byenay*	Are you free next Wednesday?
Quizá otro día. *keethah ohtroh deeyah*	Maybe another day.

la invitada
lah inbeetadah
guest

Cultural tip When you visit someone's house for the first time, it is customary to bring flowers or wine. If you are invited again, having seen your host's house, you can bring something a little more personal.

3 **In conversation** (3 minutes)

¿Quieres venir a comer el martes?
kyaires beneer ah komer el martes

Would you like to come to lunch on Tuesday?

Lo siento, estoy ocupada.
loh syaintoh, estoy okoopadah

I'm sorry, I'm busy.

¿Qué tal el jueves?
kay tal el hwebes

What about Thursday?

la anfitriona
lah anfeetiyonah
hostess

4 Words to remember (3 minutes)

Familiarize yourself with these words and test
yourself using the cover flap.

party	**la fiesta**
	lah fyaystah
dinner party	**la cena**
	lah thenah
invitation	**la invitación**
	lah inbeetathyon
reception	**la recepción**
	lah rrethepthyon
cocktail party	**el coctel**
	el koktel

5 Put into practice (5 minutes)

Join this conversation, replying in Spanish.

¿Puede venir a una   **Sí, encantado/-a.**
recepción esta noche?   *see, enkan-tadoh/-ah*
pweday beneer ah oonah
rrethepthyon estah nochay

Can you come to a
reception tonight?

Say: Yes, I'd love to.

Empieza a las ocho.   **¿Qué me pongo?**
empyaythah ah las ochoh   *kay may pongoh*

It starts at eight o'clock.

Ask: What should I wear?

Gracias por invitarnos.
grathyas por inbeetarnos
Thank you for inviting us.

Encantada.
enkan-tadah

I'd be delighted.

Ven con tu marido.
ben kon too mareedoh

Bring your husband.

Gracias, ¿a qué hora?
grathyas, ah kay orah

Thank you. What time?

REPASE Y REPITA
Review and repeat

1 Animals

❶ **el pez**
   el peth

❷ **el pájaro**
   el paharoh

❸ **el conejo**
   el konehoh

❹ **el gato**
   el gatoh

❺ **el hámster**
   el hamster

❻ **el perro**
   el perroh

1 Animals (3 minutes)

Name the numbered
animals in Spanish.

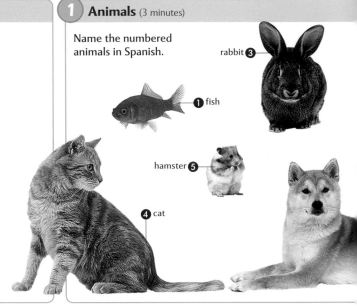

rabbit ❸

❶ fish

hamster ❺

❹ cat

2 I like...

❶ **Me gusta el fútbol.**
   may goostah el footbol

❷ **No me gusta el golf.**
   *noh may goostah
   el golf*

❸ **Me gusta pintar.**
   may goostah peentar

❹ **No me gustan
   las flores.**
   *noh may goostan
   las flores*

2 I like... (4 minutes)

Say the following in Spanish:

❶ I like soccer.
❷ I don't like golf.
❸ I like painting.
❹ I don't like flowers.

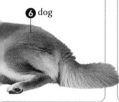

2 bird

6 dog

3 Hacer (4 minutes)

Use the correct form of the verb **hacer** (*to do* or *to make*) in these sentences.

1 Vosotros _____ senderismo.

2 Ella _____ eso todos los días.

3 ¿Qué _____ tú?

4 Hoy no _____ frío.

5 ¿Qué _____ ellos esta noche?

6 Yo _____ natación.

3 Hacer

1 hacéis
ahthays

2 hace
ahthay

3 haces
ahthes

4 hace
ahthay

5 hacen
ahthen

6 hago
ahgoh

4 An invitation (4 minutes)

You are invited for dinner. Join in the conversation, replying in Spanish following the English prompts.

¿Quieres venir a comer el viernes?
1 I'm sorry, I'm busy.

¿Qué tal el sábado?
2 I'd love to.

Ven con los niños.
3 Thank you. What time?

A las doce y media.
4 That's good for me.

4 An invitation

1 Lo siento, estoy ocupado/-a.
loh syentoh, estoy okoopadoh/-ah

2 Encantado/-a.
enkantadoh/-ah

3 Gracias. ¿A qué hora?
grathyas. ah kay orah

4 Me viene bien.
may byenay byen

Reinforce and progress

Regular practice is the key to maintaining and advancing your language skills. In this section you will find a variety of suggestions for reinforcing and extending your knowledge of Spanish. Many involve returning to exercises in the book and using the dictionaries to extend their scope. Go back through the lessons in a different order, mix and match activities to make up your own 15-minute daily program, or focus on topics that are of particular relevance to your current needs.

1 Warm up (1 minute)

Say "he is" and "they are." (pp.14–15)

Say "he is not" and "they are not." (pp.14–15)

What is Spanish for "the children"? (pp.10–11)

Keep warmed up
Revisit the Warm Up boxes to remind yourself of key words and phrases. Make sure you work your way through all of them on a regular basis.

3 I'd like... (3 minutes)

Say "I'd like" the following:

❶ black coffee   churros **❷**   **❸** sugar

coffee with milk **❹**

Review and repeat again
Work through a Review and Repeat lesson as a way of reinforcing words and phrases presented in the course. Return to the main lesson for any topic on which you are no longer confident.

3 In conversation: taxi (2 minutes)

Carry on conversing
Reread the In Conversation panels. Say both parts of the conversation, paying attention to the pronunciation. Where possible, try incorporating new words from the dictionary.

A la Plaza de España, por favor.
ah lah plathah day espanyah, por fabor

Plaza de España, please.

Sí, de acuerdo, señor.
see, day akwairdo, senyor

Yes, certainly, sir.

¿Me puede dejar aquí, por favor?
may pweday dehar ahkee, por fabor

Can you drop me here, please?

3 Useful phrases (5 minutes)

Practice these phrases and then test yourself using the cover flap.

The room is too cold/hot.	**Hace demasiado frío/calor en la habitación.** *ahthay daymasyahdoh freeoh/kalor en lah abeetathyon*
There are no towels.	**No hay toallas.** *noh ah-ee toh-ahyas*
I need some soap.	**Necesito jabón.** *netheseetoh habon*
The shower doesn't work.	**La ducha no funciona.** *lah doochah noh foonthyonah*

Practice phrases
Return to the Useful Phrases and Put into Practice exercises. Test yourself using the cover flap. When you are confident, devise your own versions of the phrases, using new words from the dictionary.

Match, repeat, and extend
Remind yourself of words related to specific topics by returning to the Match and Repeat and Words to Remember exercises. Test yourself using the cover flap. Discover new words in that area by referring to the dictionary and menu guide.

grapes **4**
mushrooms **3**
beans **2**

2 **Match and repeat** (4 minutes)

1 tomatoes   peppers **8**

Match the numbered items in this scene with the text in the panel.

1 los tomates
los to*mates*

2 las judías
las hoo*dee*as

3 los champiñones
los champeen*yones*

4 las uvas
las *oo*bas

5 los pepinos
los pe*pee*nos

6 las alcachofas
las alka*chofas*

7 los guisantes
los ghee*santes*

8 los pimientos
los peem*yaintos*

5 cucumbers

artichokes **6**   peas **7**

5 **Say it** (2 minutes)

Two kilos of peas, please.

The mushrooms are too expensive.

How much are the grapes?

Say it again
The Say It exercises are a useful instant reminder for each lesson. Practice these, using your own vocabulary variations from the dictionary or elsewhere in the lesson.

Using other resources

In addition to working with this book, try the following language extension ideas:

Visit a Spanish-speaking country and try out your new skills with native speakers. Find out if there is a Spanish community near you. There may be shops, cafés, restaurants, and clubs. Try to visit some of these and use your Spanish to order food and drink and strike up conversations. Most native speakers will be happy to speak Spanish to you.

Join a language class or club. There are usually evening and day classes available at a variety of different levels. Or you could start a club yourself if you have friends who are also interested in keeping up their Spanish.

Look at Spanish magazines and newspapers. The pictures will help you to understand the text. Advertisements are also a useful way of expanding your vocabulary.

Use the Internet, where you can find all kinds of websites for learning languages, some of which offer free online help and activities. You can also find Spanish websites for everything from renting a house to shampooing your pet. You can even access Spanish radio and TV stations online. Start by going to a Spanish search engine, such as ozu.es, and keying in a hobby or sport that interests you, or set yourself a challenge, such as finding a two-bedroom house for rent in Madrid.

MENU GUIDE

This guide lists the most common terms you may encounter on Spanish menus or when shopping for food. If you can't find an exact phrase, try looking up its component parts.

A

aceitunas *olives*
acelgas *spinach beet*
achicoria *chicory*
aguacate *avocado*
ahumados *smoked*
agua mineral *mineral water*
ajo *garlic*
al ajillo *with garlic*
a la parrilla *grilled*
a la plancha *grilled*
albaricoques *apricots*
albóndigas *meatballs*
alcachofas *artichokes*
alcaparras *capers*
al horno *baked*
allioli *garlic mayonnaise*
almejas *clams*
almejas a la marinera *clams stewed in wine and parsley*
almejas naturales *live clams*
almendras *almonds*
almíbar *syrup*
alubias *beans*
ancas de rana *frogs' legs*
anchoas *anchovies*
anguila *eel*
angulas *baby eels*
arenque *herring*
arroz a la cubana *rice with fried eggs and banana fritters*
arroz a la valenciana *rice with seafood*
arroz con leche *rice pudding*
asados *roast meat*
atún *tuna*
azúcar *sugar*

B

bacalao a la vizcaína *cod served with ham, peppers, and chili pepper*
bacalao al pil pil *cod served with chili pepper and garlic*
batido *milk shake*
bebidas *drinks*
berenjenas *eggplant*
besugo al horno *baked sea bream*
bistec de ternera *veal steak*

bonito *fish similar to tuna*
boquerones fritos *fried fresh anchovies*
brazo gitano *swiss roll*
brocheta de riñones *kidney kebabs*
buñuelos *fried pastries*
butifarra *Catalan sausage*

C

cabrito asado *roast kid*
cacahuetes *peanuts*
cachelada *pork stew with eggs, tomato, and onion*
café *coffee*
café con leche *coffee with steamed milk*
calabacines *zucchini*
calabaza *pumpkin*
calamares a la romana *squid rings in batter*
calamares en su tinta *squid cooked in their ink*
caldeirada *fish soup*
caldereta gallega *vegetable stew*
caldo de ... ... *soup*
caldo de gallina *chicken soup*
caldo de pescado *clear fish soup*
caldo gallego *vegetable soup*
caldo guanche *soup of potatoes, tomatoes, onions, and zucchini*
callos a la madrileña *tripe with chili pepper*
camarones *baby shrimp*
canela *cinnamon*
cangrejos *crabs*
caracoles *snails*
caramelos *sweets*
carnes *meats*
castañas *chestnuts*
cebolla *onion*
cebolletas *green onions*
centollo *spider crab*
cerdo *pork*
cerezas *cherries*
cerveza *beer*
cesta de frutas *selection of fresh fruit*
champiñones *mushrooms*
chanquetes *fish (similar to whitebait)*

chipirones *baby squid*
chipirones en su tinta *squid cooked in their ink*
chocos *cuttlefish*
chorizo *spicy sausage*
chuleta de buey *beef chop*
chuleta de cerdo *pork chop*
chuleta de cerdo empanada *breaded pork chop*
chuleta de cordero *lamb chop*
chuleta de cordero empanada *breaded lamb chop*
chuleta de ternera *veal chop*
chuleta de ternera empanada *breaded veal chop*
chuletas de lomo ahumado *smoked pork chops*
chuletitas de cordero *small lamb chops*
chuletón *large chop*
chuletón de buey *large beef chop*
churros *deep-fried pastry strips*
cigalas *crayfish*
cigalas cocidas *boiled crayfish*
ciruelas *plums*
ciruelas pasas *prunes*
cochinillo asado *roast suckling pig*
cocido *meat, chickpea, and vegetable stew*
cocktail de bogavante *lobster cocktail*
cocochas (de merluza) *hake stew*
cóctel de gambas *shrimp cocktail*
cóctel de langostinos *jumbo shrimp cocktail*
cóctel de mariscos *seafood cocktail*
codornices *quail*
codornices escabechadas *marinated quail*
codornices estofadas *braised quail*
col *cabbage*
coles de Bruselas *Brussels sprouts*
coliflor *cauliflower*
coñac *brandy*
conejo *rabbit*

conejo encebollado *rabbit with onions*
congrio *conger eel*
consomé con yema *consommé with egg yolk*
consomé de ave *fowl consommé*
contra de ternera con guisantes *veal stew with peas*
contrafilete de ternera *veal fillet*
copa *glass (of wine)*
copa de helado *ice cream, assorted flavors*
cordero asado *roast lamb*
cordero chilindrón *lamb stew with onion, tomato, peppers, and eggs*
costillas de cerdo *pork ribs*
crema catalana *crème brûlée*
cremada *dessert made with egg, sugar, and milk*
crema de... *cream of ... soup*
crema de legumbres *cream of vegetable soup*
crepe imperiale *crêpe suzette*
criadillas de tierra *truffles*
crocante *ice cream with chopped nuts*
croquetas *croquettes*
cuajada *curds*

D, E

dátiles *dates*
embutidos *sausages*
embutidos de la tierra *local sausages*
empanada gallega *fish pie*
empanada santiaguesa *fish pie*
empanadillas *small pies*
endivia *endive*
en escabeche *marinated*
ensalada *salad*
ensalada de arenque *fish salad*
ensalada ilustrada *mixed salad*
ensalada mixta *mixed salad*
ensalada simple *green salad*
ensaladilla rusa *Russian salad (potatoes, carrots, peas, and other vegetables in mayonnaise)*
entrecot a la parrilla *grilled entrecôte*
entremeses *hors d'oeuvres, appetizers*
escalope a la milanesa *breaded veal with cheese*
escalope a la parrilla *grilled veal*
escalope a la plancha *grilled veal*
escalope de lomo de cerdo *escalope of pork fillet*
escalope de ternera *veal escalope*

escalope empanado *breaded escalope*
escalopines al vino de Marsala *veal escalopes cooked in Marsala wine*
escalopines de ternera *veal escalopes*
espadín a la toledana *kebab*
espaguetis *spaghetti*
espárragos *asparagus*
espárragos trigueros *wild green asparagus*
espinacas *spinach*
espinazo de cerdo con patatas *stew of pork ribs with potatoes*
estofado *braised; stew*
estragón *tarragon*

F

fabada (asturiana) *bean stew with sausage*
faisán *pheasant*
faisán trufado *pheasant with truffles*
fiambres *cold meats*
fideos *thin pasta, noodles*
filete a la parrilla *grilled beef steak*
filete de cerdo *pork steak*
filete de ternera *veal steak*
flan *crème caramel*
frambuesas *raspberries*
fresas *strawberries*
fritos *fried*
fruta *fruit*

G

gallina en pepitoria *chicken stew with peppers*
gambas *shrimp*
gambas cocidas *boiled shrimp*
gambas en gabardina *shrimp in batter*
gambas rebozadas *shrimp in batter*
garbanzos *chickpeas*
garbanzos a la catalana *chickpeas with sausage, boiled eggs, and pine nuts*
gazpacho andaluz *cold tomato soup*
gelatina de ... ... *gelatin*
gratén de ... ... *au gratin (baked in a cream and cheese sauce)*
granizada *crushed ice drink*
gratinada/o *au gratin*
grelo *turnip*
grillado *grilled*
guisantes *peas*
guisantes salteados *sautéed peas*

H

habas *broad beans*
habichuelas *white beans*
helado *ice cream*
helado de vainilla *vanilla ice cream*
helado de turrón *nougat ice cream*
hígado *liver*
hígado de ternera *calves' liver*
hígado estofado *braised liver*
higos con miel y nueces *figs with honey and nuts*
higos secos *dried figs*
horchata (de chufas) *cold drink made from chufa nuts*
huevo hilado *egg yolk garnish*
huevos *eggs*
huevos a la flamenca *fried eggs with ham, tomato, and vegetables*
huevos cocidos *hard-boiled eggs*
huevos con patatas fritas *fried eggs and french fries*
huevos con picadillo *eggs with ground meat*
huevos duros *hard-boiled eggs*
huevos escalfados *poached eggs*
huevos pasados por agua *soft-boiled eggs*
huevos revueltos *scrambled eggs*

J

jamón *ham*
jamón con huevo hilado *ham with egg yolk garnish*
jamón serrano *cured ham*
jarra de vino *wine jug*
jerez *sherry*
jeta *pigs' cheeks*
judías verdes *green beans*
judías verdes a la española *bean stew*
judías verdes al natural *plain green beans*
jugo de ... ... *juice*

L

langosta *lobster*
langosta a la americana *lobster with brandy and garlic*
langosta a la catalana *lobster with mushrooms and ham in white sauce*
langosta fría con mayonesa *cold lobster with mayonnaise*
langostinos *jumbo shrimp*
langostinos dos salsas *jumbo shrimp cooked in two sauces*
laurel *bay leaves*
leche *milk*

leche frita *pudding made from milk and eggs*
leche merengada *cold milk with meringue*
lechuga *lettuce*
lengua de buey *ox tongue*
lengua de cordero *lambs' tongue*
lenguado a la romana *sole in batter*
lenguado meuniere *sole meunière (floured sole fried in butter)*
lentejas *lentils*
lentejas aliñadas *lentils in vinaigrette dressing*
licores *liquor, liqueur*
liebre estofada *stewed hare*
lima *lime*
limón *lemon*
lombarda *red cabbage*
lomo curado *pork loin sausage*
lonchas de jamón *sliced, cured ham*
longaniza *cooked Spanish sausage*
lubina *sea bass*
lubina a la marinera *sea bass in a parsley sauce*

M

macedonia de fruta *fruit salad*
mahonesa or **mayonesa** *mayonnaise*
Málaga *a sweet wine*
mandarinas *tangerines*
manitas de cordero *lamb shank*
manos de cerdo *pigs' feet*
manos de cerdo a la parrilla *grilled pigs' feet*
mantecadas *small sponge cakes*
mantequilla *butter*
manzanas *apples*
mariscada *cold mixed shellfish*
mariscos del día *fresh shellfish*
mariscos del tiempo *seasonal shellfish*
medallones *steaks*
media de agua *half- bottle of mineral water*
mejillones *mussels*
mejillones a la marinera *mussels in a wine sauce*
melocotón *peach*
melón *melon*
menestra de legumbres *vegetable stew*
menú de la casa *set menu*
menú del día *set menu*
merluza *hake*
merluza a la cazuela *stewed hake*

merluza al ajo arriero *hake with garlic and chili pepper*
merluza a la riojana *hake with chili pepper*
merluza a la romana *hake steaks in batter*
merluza a la vasca *hake in a garlic sauce*
merluza en salsa *hake in sauce*
merluza en salsa verde *hake in a green (parsley and wine) sauce*
merluza fría *cold hake*
merluza frita *fried hake*
mermelada *jam*
mero *grouper (fish)*
mero en salsa verde *grouper in green (garlic and parsley) sauce*
mollejas de ternera fritas *fried sweetbreads*
morcilla *blood sausage*
morcilla de carnero *mutton blood sausage*
morros de cerdo *pigs' cheeks*
morros de vaca *cows' cheeks*
mortadela *salami-type sausage*
morteruelo *kind of pâté*

N, O

nabo *turnip*
naranjas *oranges*
nata *cream*
natillas *cold custard*
níscalos *wild mushrooms*
nueces *walnuts*
orejas de cerdo *pigs' ears*

P

paella *fried rice with seafood and/or meat*
paella castellana *meat paella*
paella valenciana *shellfish, rabbit, and chicken paella*
paleta de cordero lechal *shoulder of lamb*
pan *bread*
panache de verduras *vegetable stew*
panceta *bacon*
parrillada de caza *mixed grilled game*
parrillada de mariscos *mixed grilled shellfish*
pasas *raisins*
pastel de ternera *veal pie*
pasteles *cakes*
patatas a la pescadora *potatoes with fish*
patatas asadas *baked potatoes*
patatas bravas *potatoes in spicy tomato sauce*
patatas fritas *french fries*
patitos rellenos *stuffed duckling*

pato a la naranja *duck in orange sauce*
pavo *turkey*
pavo trufado *turkey stuffed with truffles*
pecho de ternera *breast of veal*
pechuga de pollo *breast of chicken*
pepinillos *pickles*
pepino *cucumber*
peras *pears*
percebes *edible barnacle*
perdices a la campesina *partridges with vegetables*
perdices a la manchega *partridges in red wine, garlic, herbs, and pepper*
perdices escabechadas *marinated partridges*
perejil *parsley*
perritos calientes *hot dogs*
pescaditos fritos *fried fish*
pestiños *sugared pastries flavored with aniseed*
pez espada *swordfish*
picadillo de ternera *ground veal*
pimienta *black pepper*
pimientos *peppers*
pimientos a la riojana *baked red peppers fried in oil and garlic*
pimientos morrones *a type of bell pepper*
pimientos verdes *green peppers*
piña al gratín *pineapple au gratin*
piña fresca *fresh pineapple*
pinchitos/pinchos *kebabs, snacks served in bars*
pinchos morunos *pork kebabs*
piñones *pine nuts*
pisto *ratatouille*
pisto manchego *vegetable marrow with onion and tomato*
plátanos *bananas*
plátanos flameados *flambéed bananas*
pollo *chicken*
pollo a la riojana *chicken with peppers and chili pepper*
pollo al ajillo *fried chicken with garlic*
pollo asado *roast chicken*
pollo braseado *braised chicken*
pollo en cacerola *chicken casserole*
pollo en pepitoria *chicken in wine with saffron, garlic, and almonds*
pollos tomateros con zanahorias *young chicken with carrots*
pomelo *grapefruit*
potaje castellano *thick broth*
potaje de ... *... stew*

puchero canario *casserole of meat, chickpeas, and corn*
pulpitos con cebolla *baby octopus with onions*
pulpo *octopus*
puré de patatas *mashed potatoes, potato purée*
purrusalda *cod with leeks and potatoes*

Q

queso con membrillo *cheese with quince jelly*
queso de bola *Dutch cheese*
queso de Burgos *soft white cheese*
queso del país *local cheese*
queso de oveja *sheep's cheese*
queso gallego *a creamy cheese*
queso manchego *a hard, strong cheese*
quisquillas *shrimp*

R

rábanos *radishes*
ragout de ternera *veal ragoût*
rape a la americana *monkfish with brandy and herbs*
rape a la cazuela *stewed monkfish*
raya *skate*
rebozado *in batter*
redondo al horno *roast fillet of beef*
rellenos *stuffed*
remolacha *beet*
repollo *cabbage*
repostería de la casa *cakes baked on the premises*
requesón *cream cheese, cottage cheese*
revuelto de ... *scrambled eggs with ...*
revuelto de ajos tiernos *scrambled eggs with spring garlic*
revuelto de trigueros *scrambled eggs with asparagus*
revuelto mixto *scrambled eggs with mixed vegetables*
riñones *kidneys*
rodaballo *turbot (fish)*
romero *rosemary*
ron *rum*
roscas *sweet pastries*

S

sal *salt*
salchichas *sausages*
salchichas de Frankfurt *hot dog-type sausages*

salchichón *sausage similar to salami*
salmón ahumado *smoked salmon*
salmonetes *red mullet*
salmonetes en papillote *red mullet cooked in foil*
salmón frío *cold salmon*
salmorejo *sauce of bread, tomatoes, oil, vinegar, green pepper, and garlic*
salpicón de mariscos *shellfish in vinaigrette*
salsa *sauce*
salsa bechamel *white sauce*
salsa holandesa *hollandaise sauce*
sandía *watermelon*
sardinas a la brasa *barbecued sardines*
seco *dry*
semidulce *medium-sweet*
sesos *brains*
sesos a la romana *fried brains in batter*
sesos rebozados *brains in batter*
setas *mushrooms*
sidra *cider*
sobreasada *sausage with cayenne pepper*
solomillo *fillet steak*
solomillo con patatas *fillet steak with fries*
solomillo de ternera *fillet of veal*
solomillo de vaca *fillet of beef*
solomillo frío *cold roast beef*
sopa *soup*
sopa castellana *vegetable soup*
sopa de almendras *almond soup*
sopa de cola de buey *oxtail soup*
sopa de gallina *chicken soup*
sopa del día *soup of the day*
sopa de legumbres *vegetable soup*
sopa de marisco *fish and shellfish soup*
sopa de rabo de buey *oxtail soup*
sopa mallorquina *soup of tomato, meat, and eggs*
sopa sevillana *fish and mayonnaise soup*
soufflé de fresones *strawberry soufflé*

T

tallarines *noodles*
tallarines a la italiana *tagliatelle*

tarta *cake*
tarta de la casa *cake baked on the premises*
tarta de manzana *apple tart*
tencas *tench*
ternera asada *roast veal*
tocinillos del cielo *a very sweet crème caramel*
tomates *tomatoes*
tomillo *thyme*
torrijas *sweet pastries*
tortilla a la paisana *vegetable omelet*
tortilla a su gusto *omelet made to the customer's specifications*
tortilla de escabeche *fish omelet*
tortilla española *Spanish omelet with potato, onion, and garlic*
tortilla sacromonte *vegetable, brains, and sausage omelet*
tortillas variadas *assorted omelets*
tournedó *fillet steak*
trucha *trout*
trucha ahumada *smoked trout*
trucha escabechada *marinated trout*
truchas a la marinera *trout in wine sauce*
truchas molinera *trout meunière (floured trout fried in butter)*
trufas *truffles*
turrón *nougat*

U, V

uvas *grapes*
verduras *vegetables*
vieiras *scallops*
vino de mesa/blanco / rosado/tinto *table/ white/rosé/ red wine*

Z

zanahorias a la crema *creamed carrots*
zarzuela de mariscos *seafood stew*
zarzuela de pescados y mariscos *fish and shellfish stew*
zumo de ... ... *juice*

DICTIONARY
English to Spanish

The gender of a Spanish noun is indicated by the word for *the*: **el** and **la** (masculine and feminine singular) or their plural forms **los** (masculine) and **las** (feminine). Spanish adjectives (adj) vary according to the gender and number of the word they describe, and the masculine form is shown here. In general, adjectives that end in **-o** adopt an **-a** ending in the feminine form, and those that end in **-e** usually stay the same. For the plural form, an **-s** is added.

A

a un/una
able: to be able **poder**
about: about sixteen **alrededor de dieciséis**
accelerator **el acelerador**
accident **el accidente**
accommodation **el alojamiento**
accountant **el/la contable**
ache **el dolor**
adapter **el adaptador**
address **la dirección**
adhesive **el pegamento**
admission charge **el precio de entrada**
after ... **después de ...**
aftershave **el after-shave**
again **otra vez**
against **contra**
agenda **el orden del día**
agency **la agencia**
AIDS **el Sida**
air **el aire**
air conditioning **el aire acondicionado**
aircraft **el avión**
airline **la compañía aérea**
air mail **por avión**
air mattress **la colchoneta**
airport **el aeropuerto**
airport bus **el autobús del aeropuerto**
aisle **el pasillo**
alarm clock **el despertador**
alcohol **el alcohol**
Algeria **Argelia**
all **todo;** *all the streets* **todas las calles;** *that's all* **eso es todo**
allergic **alérgico**
almost **casi**
alone **solo**
already **ya**
always **siempre**
am: I am **soy/estoy**

ambulance **la ambulancia**
America **América**
American **el americano/ la americana**
and **y;** *(after "i" or "h")* **e**
ankle **el tobillo**
another **otro**
answering machine **el contestador automático**
antifreeze **el anticongelante**
antique shop **el anticuario**
antiseptic **el antiséptico**
apartment **el apartamento, el piso**
aperitif **el aperitivo**
appetite **el apetito**
apple **la manzana**
application form **el impreso de solicitud**
appointment (business) **la cita;** *(at hairdresser)* **hora**
apricot **el albaricoque**
April **abril**
are: you are (informal singular) **eres/estás;** *(formal singular)* **es/está;** *(informal plural)* **sois/ estáis;** *(formal plural)* **son/están;** *we are* **somos/ estamos;** *they are* **son/están**
arm **el brazo**
arrive **llegar**
art **el arte**
art gallery **la galería de arte**
artichoke **la alcachofa**
artist **el/la artista**
as: as soon as possible **lo antes posible**
ashtray **el cenicero**
asleep: he's asleep **está dormido**
aspirin **la aspirina**
asthmatic **asmático**

at: at the post office **en Correos;** *at night* **por la noche;** *at 3 o'clock* **a las tres**
athletic shoes **los zapatos de deporte**
Atlantic Ocean **el Océano Atlántico**
ATM **el cajero automático**
attic **el ático**
attractive (person) **guapo;** *(object)* **bonito;** *(offer)* **atractivo**
August **agosto**
aunt **la tía**
Australia **Australia**
Australian **el australiano/ la australiana;** *(adj)* **australiano**
automatic **automático**
available **disponible**
away: is it far away? **¿está lejos?;** *go away!* **¡váyase!**
awful **horrible**
axe **el hacha**
axle **el eje**

B

baby **el niño pequeño, el bebé**
baby carriage **el cochecito**
baby wipes **las toallitas para bebé**
back (not front) **la parte de atrás;** *(body)* **la espalda**
backpack **la mochila**
bacon **el bacon;** *bacon and eggs* **los huevos fritos con bacon**
bad **malo**
bag **la bolsa**
bait **el cebo**
bake **cocer al horno**
bakery **la pastelería**
balcony **el balcón**

Balearic Islands **las** (Islas) **Baleares**
ball (soccer) **el balon;** (tennis, etc.) **la pelota**
ballpoint pen **el bolígrafo**
banana **el plátano**
band (musicians) **la banda**
bandage **la venda;** (adhesive) **la tirita**
bangs (hair) **el flequillo**
bank **el banco**
bank card **la tarjeta de banco**
banknote **el billete de banco**
bar (drinks) **el bar**
barbecue **la barbacoa**
barber **la peluquería de caballeros**
bargain **la ganga**
basement **el sótano, la bodega**
basin (sink) **el lavabo**
basket **el cesto**
basketball **el baloncesto**
bath **el baño;** *to have a bath* **darse un baño**
bathroom **el cuarto de baño**
battery (car) **la batería;** (flashlight, etc.) **la pila**
Bay of Biscay **el Golfo de Vizcaya**
be **ser/estar**
beach **la playa**
beach ball **el balón de playa**
beans **las judías**
beard **la barba**
beautiful (object) **precioso;** (person) **guapo**
beauty products **los productos de belleza**
because **porque**
bed **la cama**
bed linen **la ropa de cama**
bedroom **el dormitorio**
bedside lamp **la lamparilla de noche**
bedspread **la colcha**
beef **la carne de vaca**
beer **la cerveza**
before ... **antes de ...**
beginner **el/la principiante**
behind ... **detrás de ...**
beige **beige**
bell (church) **la campana;** (door) **el timbre**
below **debajo de**
belt **el cinturón**
beside **al lado de**
best **(el) mejor**
better **mejor**

between **entre**
bicycle **la bicicleta**
big **grande**
bill **la cuenta**
bird **el pájaro**
birthday **el cumpleaños,** *happy birthday!* **¡felicidades!**
birthday present **el regalo de cumpleaños**
bite (by dog) **la mordedura;** (by insect) **la picadura;** (verb: by dog) **morder;** (by insect) **picar**
black **negro**
blackberries **las moras**
black currants **las grosellas negras**
blanket **la manta**
bleach **la lejía;** (verb: hair) **teñir**
blind (cannot see) **ciego**
blinds **las persianas**
blister **la ampolla**
blizzard **la ventisca**
blond (e) (adj) **rubio**
blood **la sangre**
blood test **el análisis de sangre**
blouse **la blusa**
blue **azul**
boarding pass **la tarjeta de embarque**
boat **el barco;** (small) **la barca**
body **el cuerpo**
boil (verb: water) **hervir;** (egg, etc.) **cocer**
boiled **hervido**
bolt (on door) **el cerrojo;** (verb) **echar el cerrojo**
bone **el hueso**
book **el libro;** (verb) **reservar**
bookstore **la librería**
boot (footwear) **la bota**
border **el borde;** (between countries) **la frontera**
boring **aburrido**
born: I was born in ... **nací en ...**
both: both of them **los dos;** *both of us* **los dos;** *both ... and ...* **tanto ... como ...**
bottle **la botella**
bottle opener **el abrebotellas**
bottom **el fondo;** (part of body) **el trasero**
bowl **el cuenco**
box **la caja**
box office **la taquilla**
boy **el chico**

boyfriend **el novio**
bra **el sostén**
bracelet **la pulsera**
brake **el freno;** (verb) **frenar**
branch (of company) **la oficina**
brandy **el coñac**
bread **el pan**
bread shop **la panadería**
breakdown (car) **la avería;** (nervous) **la crisis nerviosa;** *I've had a breakdown* (car) **he tenido una avería**
breakfast **el desayuno**
breathe **respirar**
bridge **el puente;** (game) **el bridge**
briefcase **la cartera**
British **británico**
brochure **el folleto**
broken **roto**
brooch **el broche**
brother **el hermano**
brown **marrón;** (hair) **castaño;** (skin) **moreno**
bruise **el cardenal**
brush (paint) **la brocha;** (cleaning) **el cepillo;** (hair) **el cepillo del pelo;** (verb: hair) **cepillar el pelo**
budget **el presupuesto**
bucket **el cubo**
building **el edificio**
bull **el toro**
bullfight **la corrida de toros**
bullfighter **el torero**
bullring **la plaza de toros**
bumper **el parachoques**
burglar **el ladrón**
burn **la quemadura;** (verb) **quemar**
bus **el autobús**
business **el negocio;** *it's none of your business* **no es asunto suyo**
business card **la tarjeta de vista**
bus station **la estación de autobuses**
busy (bar) **concurrido;** (phone) **ocupado**
but **pero**
butcher shop **la carnicería**
butter **la mantequilla**
button **el botón**
buy **comprar**
by: by the window **junto a la ventana;** *by Friday* **para el viernes;** *by myself* **yo solo;** *written by* **escrito por**

C

cabbage la col
cable car el teleférico
cable TV la television
    por cable
café el café
cage la jaula
cake (small) el pastel;
    (large) la tarta;
    sponge cake el bizcocho
calculator la calculadora
call: what's it called?
    ¿cómo se llama?
camcorder la videocámara
camera la máquina de
    fotos, la cámara de fotos
camper trailer la roulotte
camper van la autocaravana
campfire la hoguera
campground el camping
camshaft el árbol de levas
can (tin) la lata; (verb: to be
    able) poder; can you ...?
    ¿puede ...?; I can't ...
    no puedo ...
Canada Canadá
Canadian canadiense
canal el canal
Canaries las (Islas) Canarias
candle la vela
candy los caramelos (m)
can opener el abrelatas
cap (bottle) el tapón;
    (hat) la gorra
car el coche
car (train) el vagón
carburetor el carburador
card la tarjeta
cardigan sweater la rebeca
careful prudente; be careful!
    ¡cuidado!
caretaker el portero,
    el encargado
carpenter el carpintero
carpet la alfombra
carrot la zanahoria
carry-on luggage
    el equipaje de mano
car seat (for baby/child)
    el asiento infantil
cart el carrito
case (suitcase) la maleta
cash el dinero; cobrar
    (verb); to pay cash
    pagar al contado
cashier el cajero
cassette la cassette, la cinta
cassette player el cassette
castanets las castañuelas
Castile Castilla

Castilian castellano
castle el castillo
cat el gato
Catalonia Cataluña
catch (bus, etc.) coger
cathedral la catedral
Catholic (adj) católico
cauliflower la coliflor
cave la cueva
CD el disco compacto
ceiling el techo
cell phone
    el teléfono móvil,
    el teléfono celular
cemetery el cementerio
central heating
    la calefacción central
center el centro
certificate el certificado
chair la silla
change (money) el cambio;
    (verb: money) cambiar;
    (clothes) cambiarse;
    (trains, etc.) hacer
    transbordo
charger el cargador
check el cheque
checkbook
    el talonario de cheques
check-in (desk)
    la (el mostrador de)
    facturación
check in (verb) facturar
checkout (supermarket)
    la caja
cheers! (toast) ¡salud!
cheese el queso
cherry la cereza
chess el ajedrez
chest (part of body)
    el pecho; (furniture)
    el arcón
chest of drawers la cómoda
chewing gum el chicle
chicken el pollo
child el niño/la niña
children los niños
children's ward
    la sala de pediatría
chimney la chimenea
china la porcelana
chips las patatas fritas
chocolate el chocolate;
    box of chocolates la caja de
    bombones; chocolate bar
    la tableta de chocolate
chop (food) la chuleta;
    (verb: cut) cortar
Christmas la navidad
church la iglesia
cigar el puro

cigarette el cigarrillo
city la ciudad
class la clase
classical music
    la música clásica
clean (adj) limpio
cleaner la asistenta
clear (obvious)
    evidente; (water)
    claro
clever listo
client el cliente
clock el reloj
close (near) cerca
close (verb) cerrar
closed cerrado
clothes la ropa
clubs (cards) tréboles
coat el abrigo
coat hanger la percha
cockroach la cucaracha
cocktail party el coctel
coffee el café
coin la moneda
cold (illness) el resfriado;
    (adj) frío; I have a cold
    tengo un resfriado;
    I'm cold tengo frío
collar el cuello; (of animal)
    el collar
collection (stamps, etc.)
    la colección
color el color
color film la película
    en color
comb el peine; (verb) peinar
come venir; I come from ...
    soy de ...; we came last
    week llegamos la semana
    pasada; come here!
    ¡venga aquí!
come back volver
comforter el edredón
compartment
    el compartimento
complicated complicado
computer el ordenador
computer games
    los vídeo-juegos
concert el concierto
conditioner (hair)
    el acondicionador
condom el condón
conductor (bus) el cobrador;
    (orchestra) el director
conference la conferencia
conference room la sala
    de conferencias
congratulations!
    ¡enhorabuena!
consulate el consulado

contact lenses **las lentes de contacto**
contraceptive **el anticonceptivo**
contract **el contrato**
cook **el cocinero/ la cocinera;** (verb) **guisar**
cookie **la galleta**
cooking utensils **los utensilios de cocina**
cool **fresco**
cork **el corcho**
corkscrew **el sacacorchos**
corner (of street) **la esquina;** (of room) **el rincón**
corridor **el pasillo**
cosmetics **los cosméticos**
cost (verb) **costar;** what does it cost? **¿cuánto cuesta?**
cotton **el algodón**
cotton balls **el algodón**
cough **la tos;** (verb) **toser**
cough drops **las pastillas para la garganta**
countertop **el mostrador**
country (state) **el país**
countryside **el campo**
cousin **el primo/la prima**
crab **el cangrejo**
cramp **el calambre**
crayfish **las cigalas**
crazy **loco**
cream (dairy) **la nata;** (lotion) **la crema**
credit card **la tarjeta de crédito**
crib **el capazo**
crowded **lleno**
cruise **el crucero**
crutches **las muletas**
cry (weep) **llorar;** (shout) **gritar**
cucumber **el pepino**
cuff links **los gemelos**
cup **la taza**
cupboard **el armario**
curlers **los rulos**
curls **los rizos**
curry **el curry**
curtain **la cortina**
cushion **el cojín**
customs **la aduana**
cut **la cortadura;** (verb) **cortar**
cycling **el ciclismo**

D

dad **papá**
dairy products **los productos lácteos**
damp **húmedo**

dance **el baile;** (verb) **bailar**
dangerous **peligroso**
dark **oscuro;** dark blue **azul oscuro**
daughter **la hija**
day **el día**
dead **muerto**
deaf **sordo**
dear (person) **querido**
December **diciembre**
deck of cards **la baraja**
decorator **el pintor**
deep **profundo**
delayed **retrasado**
deliberately **a propósito**
delicatessen **la charcutería**
delivery **la entrega**
dentist **el/la dentista**
dentures **la dentadura postiza**
deny **negar**
deodorant **el desodorante**
department **el departemento**
department store **los grandes almacenes**
departure **la salida**
departures **las salidas**
deposit **la señal**
designer **el diseñador/ la diseñadora**
desk **la mesa de escritorio**
dessert **el postre**
develop (film) **revelar**
diabetic **diabético**
diamonds (jewels) **los diamantes;** (cards) **los diamantes**
diaper **el pañal**
diarrhea **la diarrea**
dictionary **el diccionario**
die **morir**
diesel (oil) **fuel-oil;** (adj: engine) **diesel**
different **diferente;** that's different! **¡eso es distinto!;** I'd like a different one **quisiera otro distinto**
difficult **difícil**
dining room **el comedor**
dinner **la cena**
dinner party **la cena**
dirty **sucio**
disabled **minusválido**
discount **el descuento**
dish cloth **el paño de cocina**
dishwasher **el lavavajillas**
dishwashing liquid **el lavavajillas**
disposable diapers **los pañales desechables**
divorced **divorciado**
do **hacer**

dock **el muelle**
doctor **el médico/la médica**
document **el documento**
dog **el perro**
doll **la muñeca**
dollar **el dólar**
door **la puerta**
double room **la habitación doble**
doughnut **el dónut**
down **hacia abajo**
downtown **el centro**
dress **el vestido**
drink **la bebida;** (verb) **beber;** would you like something to drink? **¿quiere beber algo?**
drinking water **agua potable**
drive (verb) **conducir**
driver **el conductor**
driver's license **el carnet de conducir**
drops **las gotas**
drunk **borracho**
dry **seco;** (sherry) **fino**
dry cleaner **la tintorería**
during **durante**
duster **el trapo del polvo**
duty-free **libre de impuestos;** duty-free shop **el duty-free**

E

each (every) **cada;** 20 euros each **veinte euros cada uno**
ear (inner) **el oído;** (outer) **la oreja;** ears **las orejas**
early **temprano**
earrings **los pendientes**
east **este;** the East **el Este**
easy **fácil**
eat **comer**
egg **el huevo**
eggplant **las berenjenas**
eight **ocho**
eighteen **dieciocho**
eighty **ochenta**
either: either of them **cualquiera de ellos;** either ... or ... **o bien ... o ...**
elastic **elástico**
elbow **el codo**
electric **eléctrico**
electrician **el/la electricista**
electricity **la electricidad**
eleven **once**
else: something else **algo más;** someone else **alguien más;** somewhere else **en otro sitio**

email **el email, el correo electrónico**
email address **la dirección de email**
embarrassing **embarazoso**
embassy **la embajada**
embroidery **el bordado**
emergency **la emergencia**
emergency brake (train) **el freno de emergencia**
emergency department **el servicio de urgencias**
emergency exit **la salida de emergencia**
employee **el empleado**
empty **vacío**
end **el final**
engaged (marriage) **prometido/prometida**
engine (motor) **el motor**
engineering **la ingeniería**
England **Inglaterra**
English **inglés**
Englishman **el inglés**
Englishwoman **la inglesa**
enlargement **la ampliación**
enough **bastante**
entertainment **las diversiones**
entrance **la entrada**
envelope **el sobre**
epileptic **epiléptico**
eraser **la goma de borrar**
escalator **la escalera mecánica**
especially **sobre todo**
espresso **el café solo**
estimate **el presupuesto**
evening **la tarde**
every **cada;** *every day* **todos los días**
everyone **todos**
everything **todo**
everywhere **por todas partes**
example **el ejemplo;** *for example* **por ejemplo**
excellent **excelente**
excess baggage **exceso de equipaje**
exchange (verb) **cambiar**
exchange rate **el cambio**
excursion **la excursión**
excuse me! (to get attention) **¡oiga, por favor!;** (when sneezing, etc.) **¡perdón!;** *excuse me, please* (to get past) **¿me hace el favor?**
executive **el ejecutivo**
exhaust **el tubo de escape**
exhibition **la exposición**

exit **la salida**
expensive **caro**
expressway **la autopista**
extension cord **el cable alargador**
eye **el ojo**
eyebrow **la ceja**

F

face **la cara**
faint (unclear) **tenue;** (verb) **desmayarse;** *I feel faint* **estoy mareado**
fair **la feria;** *it's not fair* **no hay derecho**
false teeth **la dentadura postiza**
family **la familia**
fan (enthusiast) **el fan;** (soccer) **el hincha;** (ventilator) **el ventilador;** (handheld) **el abanico**
fantastic **fantástico**
far **lejos;** *how far is it to ...?* **¿qué distancia hay a ...?**
fare **el billete, la tarifa**
farm **la granja**
farmer **el granjero**
fashion **la moda**
fast **rápido**
fat (adj) **gordo;** (on meat) **la grasa**
father **el padre**
faucet **el grifo**
February **febrero**
feel (touch) **tocar;** *I feel hot* **tengo calor;** *I feel like ...* **me apetece ...;** *I don't feel well* **no me encuentro bien**
felt-tip pen **el rotulador**
fence **la cerca**
ferry **el ferry**
fiancé **el prometido**
fiancée **la prometida**
field (of grass, etc.) **el campo;** (of study) **la especialidad**
fifteen **quinze**
fifty **cincuenta**
fig **el higo**
figures **los números**
filling (in tooth) **el empaste;** (in sandwich, cake) **el relleno**
film **la película**
filter **el filtro**
filter papers **los papeles de filtro**

finger **el dedo**
fire **el fuego;** (blaze) **el incendio**
fire extinguisher **el extintor**
fireplace **la chimenea**
fireworks **los fuegos artificiales**
first **primero;** *first aid* **primeros auxilios**
first class **de primera**
first floor **el primer piso**
first name **el nombre de pila**
fish **el pez;** (food) **el pescado**
fishing **la pesca;** *to go fishing* **ir a pescar**
fishmonger **la pescadería**
five **cinco**
flag **la bandera**
flash (camera) **el flash**
flashlight **la linterna**
flat (level) **plano**
flat tire **la rueda pinchada**
flavor **el sabor**
flea **la pulga**
flea spray **el spray antipulgas**
flight **el vuelo**
floor **el suelo;** (story) **el piso**
flour **la harina**
flower **la flor**
flowerbed **el parterre**
flute **la flauta**
fly (insect) **la mosca;** (verb: of plane, insect) **volar;** (of person) **viajar en avión**
fog **la niebla**
folk music **la música folklórica**
food **la comida**
food poisoning **la intoxicación alimenticia**
foot **el pie**
for: *for me* **para mí;** *what for?* **¿para qué?;** *for a week* **(para) una semana**
foreigner **el extranjero/ la extranjera**
forest **el bosque;** (tropical) **la selva**
forget **olvidar**
fork **el tenedor;** (garden) **la horca**
forty **cuarenta**
fountain **la fuente**
fountain pen **la (pluma) estilográfica**
four **cuatro**
fourteen **catorce**
fourth **cuarto**
France **Francia**

free (not engaged) **libre**;
  (no charge) **gratis**
freezer **el congelador**
French **francés**
french fries **las patatas fritas**
Friday **viernes**
fried **frito**
friend **el amigo/la amiga**
friendly **simpático**
front: in front of ... **delante**
  de ...
frost **la escarcha**
frozen foods **los congelados**
fruit **la fruta**
fruit juice **el zumo de frutas**
fry **freír**
frying pan **la sartén**
full **lleno**; *I'm full* **estoy lleno**
full board **pensión completa**
funny **divertido**; (odd) **raro**
furniture **los muebles**

G

garage (for parking) **el**
  garage; (for repairs) **el taller**
garbage **la basura**
garbage bag **la bolsa**
  de basura
garden **el jardín**
garden center **el vivero**
garlic **el ajo**
gasoline **la gasolina**
gas-permeable lenses
  las lentes de contacto
  semi-rígidas
gas station **la gasolinera**
gate **la puerta, la verja**;
  (at airport) **la puerta**
  de embarque
gay (homosexual) **gay**
gearbox **la caja de cambios**
gear stick **la palanca**
  de velocidades
gel (hair) **el gel**
German **alemán**
Germany **Alemania**
get (fetch) **traer**; *have you*
  got ...? **¿tiene ...?**; *to get the*
  train **coger el tren**
get back: we get back tomorrow
  nos volvemos mañana;
  to get something back
  recobrar algo
get in (of train, etc.)
  subirse; (of person) **llegar**
get off (bus, etc.) **bajarse**
get on (bus, etc.) **subirse**
get out **bajarse**;
  (bring out) **sacar**
get up (rise) **levantarse**

Gibraltar **Gibraltar**
gift **el regalo**
gin **la ginebra**
ginger (spice) **el jengibre**
girl **la chica**
girlfriend **la novia**
give **dar**
glad **alegre**
glass (material) **el cristal**; (for
  drinking) **el vaso, la copa**
glasses **las gafas**
gloss prints **las copias**
  con brillo
gloves **los guantes**
glue **el pegamento**
go **ir**
gold **el oro**
good **bueno**; *good!* **¡bien!**
good afternoon
  buenas tardes
goodbye **adiós**
good evening **buenas noches**
good morning **buenos días**
government **el gobierno**
granddaughter **la nieta**
grandfather **el abuelo**
grandmother **la abuela**
grandparents **los abuelos**
grandson **el nieto**
grapes **las uvas**
grass **la hierba**
gray **gris**
Great Britain **Gran Bretaña**
green **verde**
greengrocer **la verdulería**
grill **la parrilla**
grilled **a la plancha**
grocery store
  el ultramarinos,
  la tienda de comestibles
ground floor **la planta baja**
groundsheet **la lona**
  impermeable, el
  suelo aislante
guarantee **la garantía**;
  (verb) **garantizar**
guest **la invitada**
guide **el/la guía**
guide book **la guía turística**
guided tour **la visita con guía**
guitar **la guitarra**
gun (rifle) **la escopeta**;
  (pistol) **la pistola**
gym **el centro deportivo**

H

hair **el pelo**
haircut **el corte de pelo**
hairdryer **el secador** (de pelo)
hair salon **la peluquería**

hairspray **la laca**
half **medio**; *half an hour*
  media hora
half board **media pensión**
ham **el jamón**
hamburger **la hamburguesa**
hammer **el martillo**
hamster **el hámster**
hand **la mano**
handbag **el bolso**
handbrake **el freno de mano**
handle (door) **el picaporte**
handshake
  el apretón de manos
handsome **guapo**
handyman **el albañil**
hangover **la resaca**
happy **contento, feliz**
harbor **el puerto**
hard **duro**; (difficult) **difícil**
hardware store **la ferretería**
hat **el sombrero**; (woollen)
  el gorro
have **tener**; *I don't have ...* **no**
  tengo ...; *do you have ...?*
  ¿tiene ...?; *I have to go*
  tengo que irme; *can I*
  have ...? **¿me pone ...?**
hay fever **la fiebre del heno**
he **él**
head **la cabeza**
headache **el dolor de cabeza**
headlights **los faros**
headphones **los auriculares**
hear **oír**
hearing aid **el audífono**
heart **el corazón**
hearts (cards) **los corazones**
heater **la estufa**
heating **la calefacción**
heavy **pesado**
hedge **el seto**
heel **el talón**; (shoe) **el tacón**
hello **hola**; (on phone) **dígame**
help **la ayuda**; (verb) **ayudar**
hepatitis **la hepatitis**
her: it's for her **es para ella**;
  her book **su libro**; *her shoes*
  sus zapatos; *it's hers* **es**
  suyo; *give it to her* **déselo**
high **alto**
highway code **el código**
  de la circulación
hiking **el senderismo**
hill **el monte**
him: it's for him **es para él**;
  give it to him **déselo**
his: his book **su libro**; *his shoes*
  sus zapatos; *it's his*
  es suyo
history **la historia**

hitchhike **hacer auto-stop**
HIV positive **seropositivo**
hobby **el hobby**
home **la casa;**
   at home **en casa**
homeopathy **la homeopatía**
honest **honrado;**
   (sincere) **sincero**
honey **la miel**
honeymoon **el viaje de novios**
horn (car) **el claxon;**
   (animal) **el cuerno**
hood (car) **el capó**
horrible **horrible**
hospital **el hospital**
hostess **la anfitriona**
hour **la hora**
house **la casa**
household products **los productos del hogar**
hovercraft **el aerodeslizador**
how? **¿cómo?**
how are you? **¿qué tal?**
hundred **cien**
hungry: I'm hungry **tengo hambre**
hurry: I'm in a hurry **tengo prisa**
husband **el marido**
hydrofoil **la hidroaleta**

I

I **yo**
ice **el hielo**
ice cream **el helado**
ice skates **los patines para hielo**
if **si**
ignition **el encendido**
immediately **inmediatamente**
impossible **imposible**
in **en;** in English **en inglés;**
   in the hotel **en el hotel;** in
   Barcelona **en Barcelona;**
   he's not in **no está**
included **incluido**
indigestion **indigestión**
inexpensive **barato**
infection **la infección**
information **la información**
inhaler (for asthma, etc.)
   el spray, el inhalador
injection **la inyección**
injury **la herida**
ink **la tinta**
inn **la fonda**
inner tube
   la cámara (neumática)
insect **el insecto**

insect repellent **la loción anti-mosquitos**
insomnia **el insomnio**
instant coffee
   el café instantáneo
insurance **el seguro**
interesting **interesante**
Internet **el internet**
interpret **interpretar**
interpreter **el/la intérprete**
invitation **la invitación**
invoice **la factura**
Ireland **Irlanda**
Irish **irlandés/ irlandesa**
iron (metal) **el hierro;**
   (for clothes) **la plancha;**
   (verb) **planchar**
is **es/está**
island **la isla**
it **lo/la**
Italian (adj) **italiano/ italiana** (m/f)
Italy **Italia**
its **su**

J

jacket **la chaqueta**
jam **la mermelada**
January **enero**
jazz **el jazz**
jeans **los tejanos, los vaqueros**
jellyfish **la medusa**
jeweler **la joyería**
job **el trabajo**
jog (verb) **hacer footing**
jogging suit **el chandal**
joke **la broma;** (funny story) **el chiste**
journey **el viaje**
juice **el zumo**
July **julio**
June **junio**
just (only) **sólo;** it's just arrived **acaba de llegar**

K

kerosene **la parafina**
key **la llave**
keyboard **el teclado**
kidney **el riñón**
kilo **el kilo**
kilometer **el kilómetro**
kitchen **la cocina**
knee **la rodilla**
knife **el cuchillo**
knit **hacer punto**

knitwear **los artículos de punto**
know **saber;** (person, place) **conocer;** I don't know **no sé**

L

label **la etiqueta**
lace **el encaje**
laces (shoe) **los cordones** (de los zapatos)
lady **la señora**
lake **el lago**
lamb **el cordero**
lamp **la lámpara, el flexo**
lampshade **la pantalla**
land **la tierra;** (verb) **aterrizar**
language **el idioma**
large **grande**
last (final) **último;** at last! **¡por fin!** ; last week **la semana pasada**
late: it's getting late **se está haciendo tarde;** the bus is late **el autobús se ha retrasado**
later **más tarde**
laugh **reír**
laundromat **la lavandería automática**
laundry (dirty) **la ropa sucia;** (washed) **la colada**
laundry detergent **el jabón de lavadora, el detergente**
law **el derecho**
lawn **el césped**
lawn mower **la maquina cortacésped**
lawyer **el abogado/ la abogada**
laxative **el laxante**
lazy **perezoso**
leaf **la hoja**
leaflet **el folleto**
learn **aprender**
leash **la correa**
leather **el cuero**
lecture hall **el anfiteatro**
left (not right) **izquierdo;** there's nothing left **no queda nada**
leg **la pierna**
lemon **el limón**
lemonade **la limonada**
length **la longitud**
lens **la lente**
less **menos**
lesson **la clase**
letter (mail) **la carta;** (of alphabet) **la letra**
lettuce **la lechuga**

library la biblioteca
license el permiso
license plate la matrícula
life la vida
lift el ascensor
light la luz; (weight) ligero;
  (not dark) claro
light bulb la bombilla
lighter el encendedor
lighter fuel el gas para
  el encendedor
light meter el fotometro
like: I like ... me gusta ...;
  I like swimming me gusta
  nadar; it's like ... es
  como ...; like this one
  como éste
lime (fruit) la lima
line la cola; (phone, etc.)
  línea; (verb) hacer cola
lipstick la barra de labios
liqueur el licor
list la lista
liter el litro
literature la literatura
litter la basura
little (small) pequeño; it's
  a little big es un poco
  grande; just a little sólo
  un poquito
liver el hígado
living room el cuarto
  de estar
lobster la langosta
lollipop el chupa-chups
long largo
lost property office la oficina
  de objetos perdidos
lot: a lot mucho
loud alto
lounge (in house) el cuarto
  de estar; (in hotel, etc.)
  el salón
love el amor; (verb)
  querer; I love Spain
  me encanta España
lover el/la amante
low bajo
luck: good luck! ¡suerte!
luggage el equipaje
luggage rack la rejilla
  de equipajes
lunch la comida

M

madam señora
magazine la revista
mail el correo; (verb)
  echar al correo
mailbox el buzón

mail carrier el cartero
main course
  el plato principal
main road la calle principal
Majorca Mallorca
make hacer
make-up el maquillaje
man el hombre
manager el/la gerente,
  el jefe; (hotel) el director/
  la directora
many muchos/muchas;
  many thanks muchas
  gracias; many people
  mucha gente; how many
  ¿cuántos?; too many
  demasiados; not many
  no muchos
map el mapa; town map/plan
  el plano
marble el mármol
March marzo
margarine la margarina
market el mercado
marmalade la mermelada
  de naranja
married casado
mascara el rímel
mass (church) la misa
match (light) la cerilla;
  (sports) el partido
material (cloth) la tela
matter: it doesn't matter
  no importa
mattress el colchón
May mayo
maybe quizás
me: it's for me es para mí;
  give it to me démelo
meal la comida
mean: what does this mean?
  ¿qué significa esto?
meat la carne
mechanic el mecánico
medicine la medicina
Mediterranean
  el Mediterráneo
medium (sherry) amontillado
medium-dry (wine) semi-seco
meeting la reunión
melon el melón
menu la carta; set menu
  el menú (del día)
message el recado,
  el mensaje
metro station
  le estación de metro
microwave el microondas
middle: in the middle
  en el centro
midnight medianoche

milk la leche
mine: it's mine es mío
mineral water el agua
  mineral
minute el minuto
mirror el espejo
Miss Señorita
mistake la equivocación
modem el modem
Monday lunes
money el dinero
monitor el monitor
month el mes
monument el monumento
moon la luna
moped el ciclomotor
more más
morning la mañana;
  in the morning
  por la mañana
Morocco Marruecos
mosaic el mosaico
mosquito el mosquito
mother la madre
motorboat la motora
motorcycle la motocicleta
mountain la montaña
mountain bike la bicicleta
  de montaña
mouse el ratón
mousse (for hair)
  la espuma
  moldeadora
mouth la boca
move (verb: something)
  mover; (oneself)
  moverse; (house)
  mudarse de casa;
  don't move! ¡no se
  mueva!
movie la película
movie theater el cine
Mr. Señor
Mrs. Señora
much: much better mucho
  mejor; much slower
  mucho más despacio
mug la jarrita
Mum mama
museum el museo
mushrooms los
  champiñones,
  las setas
music la música
musical instrument
  el instrumento musical
musician el músico
music system
  el equipo de música
mussels los mejillones
must (to have to)

tener que I must ...
tengo que ...
mustache el bigote
mustard la mostaza
my: my book mi libro;
    my keys mis llaves

N

nail (metal) el clavo;
    (finger) la uña
nail clippers el cortauñas
nailfile la lima de uñas
nail polish el esmalte
    de uñas
name el nombre; *what's your
    name?* ¿cómo se llama
    usted?; *my name is...*
    me llamo...
napkin la servilleta
narrow estrecho
near: near the door junto a la
    puerta; *near New York*
    cerca de New York
necessary necesario
neck el cuello
necklace el collar
need (verb) necesitar;
    I need ... necesito ...; *there's
    no need* no hace falta
needle la aguja
negative (photo) el negativo
neither: neither of them
    ninguno de ellos;
    neither ... nor ... ni ... ni ...
nephew el sobrino
never nunca
new nuevo
news las noticias
newspaper el periódico
newsstand el kiosko
    de periódicos
New Zealand Nueva Zelanda
New Zealander
    el neozelandés/
    la neozelandesa
next próximo, siguiente;
    next week la semana que
    viene; *what next?*
    ¿y ahora qué?
nice bonito; (pleasant)
    agradable; (to eat) bueno
niece la sobrina
night la noche
nightclub la discoteca
nightgown el camisón
night porter el vigilante
    nocturno
nightstand la mesilla
    de noche
nine nueve

nineteen diecinueve
ninety noventa
no (response) no; *I have no
    money* no tengo dinero
nobody nadie
noisy ruidoso
noon mediodía
north el norte
Northern Ireland
    Irlanda del Norte
nose la nariz
not no; *he's not ...* no es/está ...
notebook el cuaderno
notepad el bloc
nothing nada
novel la novela
November noviembre
now ahora
nowhere en ninguna parte
nudist el/la nudista
number el número
nurse el enfermo/
    la enfermera
nut (fruit) la nuez;
    (for bolt) la tuerca

O

oars los remos
occasionally de vez
    en cuando
occupied ocupado
October octubre
octopus el pulpo
of de
office (place) la oficina;
    (room) el despacho
office block el bloque
    de oficinas
often a menudo
oil el aceite
ointment la pomada
OK vale
old viejo; *how old are you?*
    ¿cuántos años tiene?
olive la aceituna
olive oil el aceite de oliva
olive tree el olivo
omelet la tortilla
on ... en ...
one uno
onion la cebolla
only sólo
open (adj) abierto;
    (verb) abrir
opening times
    el horario de apertura
operating room el quirófano
operation la operación
operator la operadora
across from: across from the

hotel enfrente del hotel
optician el/la oculista
or o
orange (fruit) la naranja;
    (color) naranja
orchestra la orquesta
order el pedido
organ (music) el órgano
other: the other (one) el otro
our nuestro; *it's ours* es nuestro
out: he's out no está
outside fuera; *external* externa
oven el horno
over ... encima de ...; (more
    than) más de ...; *it's over
    the road* está al otro lado
    de la calle; *when the party
    is over* cuando termine
    la fiesta; *over there* allí
overpass el paso elevado
oyster la ostra

P

package el paquete
packet el paquete;
    (cigarettes) la cajetilla;
    (candy, chips) la bolsa
padlock el candado
page la página
pain el dolor
paint la pintura
pair el par
pajamas el pijama
palace el palacio
pale pálido
pancakes las crepes
pants el pantalón
pantyhose las medias,
    los pantis
paper el papel; (newspaper)
    el periódico
pardon? ¿cómo dice?
parents los padres
park el parque; (verb)
    aparcar; *no parking*
    prohibido aparcar
parking lot el aparcamiento
parsley el perejil
part (hair) la raya
party (celebration)
    la fiesta; (group)
    el grupo; (political)
    el partido
passenger el pasajero
pass (in car) adelantar
passport el pasaporte
password la contraseña
pasta la pasta
path el camino
pavement la acera

pay **pagar**
payment **el pago**
peach **el melocotón**
peanuts **los cacahuetes**
pear **la pera**
pearl **la perla**
peas **los guisantes**
pedestrian **el peatón**
pedestrian zone
   la zona peatonal
peg **la pinza**
pen **la pluma**
pencil **el lápiz**
pencil sharpener
   el sacapuntas
penknife **la navaja**
pen pal **el amigo/**
   la amiga por
   correspondencia
people **la gente**
pepper **la pimienta;**
   (red, green) **el pimiento**
peppermints **las pastillas**
   de menta
per: per night **por noche**
perfect **perfecto**
perfume **el perfume**
perhaps **quizás**
perm **la permanente**
pet passport **el pasaporte**
   de animales
pets **los animales de**
   compañía; los animales
   domésticos
pharmacy **la farmacia**
phone book **la guía**
   telefónica
phone booth
   la cabina telefónica
phone card
   la tarjeta telefónica
photocopier **la fotocopiadora**
photograph **la foto**(grafía);
   (verb) **fotografiar**
photographer **el fotógrafo**
phrase book **el libro**
   de frases
piano **el piano**
pickpocket **el carterista**
pickup (postal) **la recogida**
picnic **el picnic**
piece **el pedazo**
pill **la pastilla**
pillow **la almohada**
pilot **el piloto**
PIN **el pin**
pin **el alfiler**
pine (tree) **el pino**
pineapple **la piña**
pink **rosa**
pipe (for smoking) **la pipa;**

(for water) **la tubería**
piston **el piston**
pizza **la pizza**
place **el lugar;** *at your place*
   en su casa
planner **la agenda**
plant **la planta**
plastic **el plástico**
plastic bag **la bolsa**
   de plástico
plastic wrap **el plástico**
   para envolver
plate **el plato**
platform (train) **el andén**
play (theater) **la obra de**
   teatro; *(verb)* **jugar**
please **por favor**
pleased to meet you
   encantado/encantada
plug (electrical) **el enchufe;**
   (sink) **el tapón**
plumber **el fontanero/**
   la fontanera
pocket **el bolsillo**
poison **el veneno**
police **la policía**
police officer **el policía**
police report **la denuncia**
police station **la comisaría**
politics **la política**
poor **pobre;** *(bad quality)* **malo**
pop music **la música pop**
pork **la carne de cerdo**
port (harbor) **el puerto;**
   (drink) **el oporto**
porter (hotel) **el conserje**
Portugal **Portugal**
Portuguese **portugués**
possible **posible**
postcard **la postal**
poster **el póster**
post office
   (la oficina de) **Correos**
potato **la patata**
poultry **las aves**
pound (sterling) **la libra**
powder **el polvo;** *(cosmetic)*
   los polvos
prefer **preferir**
pregnant **embarazada**
prescription **la receta**
pretty **bonito;** *(quite)*
   bastante
price **el precio**
priest **el cura**
printer **la impresora**
private **privado**
problem **el problema**
profession **la profesión**
professor **el catedrático;**
professor (university)

el profesor/la profesora
   de universidad
profits **los beneficios**
prohibited **prohibido**
protection factor (SPF) **el**
   factor de protección
public **público**
public holiday **el día**
   de fiesta
public swimming pool
   la piscina municipal
pull **tirar de**
puncture **el pinchazo**
purple **morado**
purse **la cartera,**
   el monedero
push **empujar**
put **poner**
Pyrenees **los Pirineos**

Q

quality **la calidad**
quarter **el cuarto**
question **la pregunta**
quick **rápido**
quiet **tranquilo;**
   (person) **callado**
quite (fairly) **bastante;**
   (fully) **completamente**

R

rabbit **el conejo**
radiator **el radiador**
radio **la radio**
radish **el rábano**
rake **el rastrillo**
railroad **el ferrocarril**
rain **la lluvia**
raincoat **la gabardina**
rainforest **la selva**
raisins **las pasas**
raspberry **la frambuesa**
rare (uncommon) **raro;**
   (steak) **poco hecho,**
   poco pasado
rat **la rata**
razor blades **las cuchillas**
   de afeitar
read **leer**
ready **listo**
receipt **el recibo**
reception **la recepción**
receptionist
   el/la recepcionista
record (music) **el disco;**
   (sports, etc.) **el récord**
record player **el tocadiscos**
record store **la tienda de discos**
red **rojo;** *(wine)* **tinto**

refreshments **los refrescos**
refrigerator **el frigorífico**
registered mail
  correo certificado
relative **el pariente**
relax **relajarse;**
  (rest) **descansar**
religion **la religión**
remember: I remember
  me acuerdo; *I don't*
  remember **no me**
  acuerdo
rent (verb) **alquilar**
repair **arreglar**
report **el informe**
reservation **la reserva**
rest (remainder) **el resto;**
  (verb: relax) **descansar**
restaurant **el restaurante**
restaurant car
  el vagón-restaurante
restrooms **los servicios**
return (come back) **volver;**
  (give back) **devolver**
rice **el arroz**
rich **rico**
right (correct) **correcto;**
  (not left) **derecho**
ring (for finger) **el anillo**
ripe **maduro**
river **el río**
road **la carretera**
roasted **asado**
robbery **el robo**
rock (stone) **la roca**
roll (bread) **el bollo**
roof **el tejado**
room **la habitación;** (space)
  el sitio
room service **el servicio**
  de habitaciones
rope **la cuerda**
rose **la rosa**
round (circular) **redondo**
roundabout **la rotonda**
round-trip ticket **el billete**
  de ida y vuelta
row (verb) **remar**
rowing boat **la barca**
  de remos
rubber (material) **la goma**
rubber band **la goma**
ruby (stone) **el rubí**
rug (mat) **la alfombra;**
  (blanket) **la manta**
rugby **el rugby**
ruins **las ruinas**
ruler (for measuring) **la regla**
rum **el ron**
run (verb) **correr**
runway **la pista**

S

sad **triste**
safe (not dangerous) **seguro**
safety pin **el imperdible**
sailboard **la tabla**
  de windsurfing
sailing **la vela**
salad **la ensalada**
sale (at reduced prices)
  las rebajas
sales **las ventas**
salmon **el salmón**
salt **la sal**
same: the same dress **el**
  mismo vestido; *the same*
  people **la misma gente;**
  same again, please **lo**
  mismo otra vez, por favor
sand **la arena**
sandals **las sandalias**
sand dunes **las dunas**
sandwich **el bocadillo**
sanitary napkins **las compresas**
Saturday **sábado**
sauce **la salsa**
saucepan **el cazo**
saucer **el platillo**
sauna **la sauna**
sausage **la salchicha**
say **decir;** *what did you say?*
  ¿qué ha dicho?; *how do*
  you say ...? **¿cómo se**
  dice ...?
scarf **la bufanda;** (head)
  el pañuelo
schedule **el programa,**
  el horario
school **la escuela**
science **las ciencias**
scissors **las tijeras**
Scotland **Escocia**
Scottish **escocés/escocesa**
screen **la pantalla**
screw **el tornillo**
screwdriver **el destornillador**
sea **el mar**
seafood **los mariscos**
seat **el asiento**
seat belt **el cinturón**
  de seguridad
second **el segundo**
second class **de segunda**
see **ver;** *I can't see* **no veo;**
  I see **comprendo**
self-employed (person) **el**
  autónomo/la autónoma
sell **vender**
seminar **el seminario**
send **mandar**
separate (adj) **distinto**

separated **separado**
September **septiembre**
serious **serio**
seven **siete**
seventeen **diecisiete**
seventy **setenta**
several **varios**
sew **coser**
shampoo **el champú**
shave **el afeitado;**
  to shave **afeitarse**
shaving foam **la espuma**
  de afeitar
shawl **el chal**
she **ella**
sheet **la sábana;**
  (of paper) **la hoja**
shell **la concha**
shellfish **mariscos**
sherry **el jerez**
ship **el barco**
shirt **la camisa**
shoelaces **los cordones**
  de los zapatos
shoe polish **la crema**
  de zapatos
shoes **los zapatos**
shoe store **la zapatería**
shopping **la compra;** *to go*
  shopping **ir de compras**
short **corto;** (height) **bajo**
shorts **los pantalones cortos**
shoulder **el hombro**
shower (bath) **la ducha;**
  (rain) **el chaparrón**
shower gel **el gel de ducha**
shrimp **las quisquillas,**
  las gambas
shutter (camera)
  el obturador; (window)
  el postigo
sick: I feel sick **tengo náuseas;**
  to be sick (vomit) **devolver**
side (edge) **el borde**
side lights **las luces**
  de posición
sights: the sights of ... **los**
  lugares de interés de ...
sightseeing **el turismo**
silk **la seda**
silver (metal) **la plata;**
  (color) **plateado**
simple **sencillo**
sing **cantar**
single (ticket) **de ida;**
  (only) **único;** (unmarried)
  soltero/soltera
single room
  la habitación *individual*
sink **el fregadero**
sister **la hermana**

six **seis**
sixteen **dieciséis**
sixty **sesenta**
skid **patinar**
skiing: to go skiing **ir a esquiar**
skin cleanser
　la leche limpiadora
ski resort **la estación**
　de esquí
skirt **la falda**
skis **los esquís**
sky **el cielo**
sleep **el sueño;** (verb) **dormir**
sleeper car **el coche-cama**
sleeping bag **el saco de dormir**
sleeping pill **el somnífero**
sleeve **la manga**
slip (underwear)
　la combinacíon
slippers **las zapatillas**
slow **lento**
small **pequeño**
smell **el olor;** (verb) **oler**
smile **la sonrisa;**
　(verb) **sonreír**
smoke **el humo;** (verb) **fumar**
snack **la comida ligera**
snow **la nieve**
so: so good **tan bueno;**
　not so much **no tanto**
soaking solution
　(for contact lenses)
　la solución limpiadora
soap **el jabón**
soccer **el fútbol;**
　(ball) **el balón**
socks **los calcetines**
soda water **la soda**
sofa **el sofa**
soft **blando**
soil **la tierra**
somebody **alguien**
somehow **de algún modo**
something **algo**
sometimes **a veces**
somewhere **en alguna**
　parte
son **el hijo**
song **la canción**
sorry! **¡perdón!;** I'm sorry
　perdón/lo siento; sorry?
　(pardon) **¿cómo dice?**
soup **la sopa**
south **el sur**
South America **Sudamérica**
souvenir **el recuerdo**
spade **la pala**
spades (cards) **las picas**
Spain **España**
Spaniard **el español/**
　la española

sparkling water **el agua**
　con gas
speak **hablar;** do you speak ...?
　¿habla ...?;
I don't speak ... **no hablo ...**
speed **la velocidad**
speed limit **el límite**
　de velocidad
spider **la araña**
spinach **las espinacas**
spoon **la cuchara**
sports **el deporte**
spring (mechanical)
　el muelle; (season)
　la primavera
square (in town)
　la plaza; (adj) **cuadrado**
staircase **la escalera**
stairs **las escaleras**
stamp **el sello**
stapler **la grapadora**
star **la estrella**
start (beginning) **el**
　principio; (verb) **empezar**
starters **los entrantes**
statement **la declaración**
station **la estación**
statue **la estatua**
steak **el filete**
steal **robar;** it's been stolen
　lo han robado
steamed **al vapor**
steamer (boat) **el vapor**
stepdaughter **la hijastra**
stepfather **el padastro**
stepmother **la madastra**
stepson **el hijastro**
still water **el agua sin gas**
stockings **las medias**
stomach **el estómago**
stomach-ache **el dolor**
　de estómago
stop (bus) **la parada;**
　(verb) **parar;** stop! **¡alto!**
store **la tienda**
storm **la tormenta**
stove **la cocina**
stove fuel **el camping-gas**
strawberries **las fresas**
stream (small river) **el arroyo**
street **la calle**
string **la cuerda**
stroller **la sillita de**
　ruedas
strong **fuerte**
student **el/la estudiante**
stuffy **sofocante**
stupid **estúpido**
suburbs **las afueras**
subway **el metro**
sugar **el azúcar**

suit (clothing) **el traje;**
　it suits you **te sienta**
　bien
suitcase **la maleta**
sun **el sol**
sunbathe **tomar el sol**
sunburn **la quemadura**
　de sol
Sunday **domingo**
sunglasses **las gafas de sol**
sunny: it's sunny **hace sol**
sunshade **la sombrilla**
sunstroke **la insolación**
suntan: to get a suntan
　broncearse
suntan lotion
　la loción bronceadora
suntanned **bronceado**
supermarket **el supermercado**
supper **la cena**
supplement **el suplemento**
suppository **el supositorio**
sure **seguro**
surname **el apellido**
suspenders (clothing)
　los tirantes
sweat **el sudor;** (verb) **sudar**
sweater **el jersey**
sweatshirt **la sudadera**
sweet (adj: not sour) **dulce**
swim (verb) **nadar**
swimming **la natación**
swimming pool **la piscina**
swimming trunks **el bañador**
swimsuit **el bañador,**
　el traje de baño
switch **el interruptor**
synagogue **la sinagoga**
syringe **la jeringuilla**
syrup **el jarabe**

T

table **la mesa**
tablet **la pastilla**
take **tomar**
take off **el despegue**
talcum powder
　los polvos de talco
talk **la charla;** (verb) **hablar**
tall **alto**
tampons **los tampones**
tangerine **la mandarina**
tapestry **el tapiz**
taxi **el taxi**
taxi stand **la parada de taxis**
tea **el té**
teakettle **el hervidor de agua**
teacher **el profesor/**
　la profesora
technician **el técnico**

telephone **el teléfono**; (verb)
  llamar por teléfono
television **la televisión**
temperature **la temperatura**;
  (fever) **la fiebre**
ten **diez**
tennis **el tenis**
tent **la tienda**
tent peg **la estaquilla,**
  la estaca
tent pole **el mástil**
terminal **la terminal**
terrace **la terraza**
test **la prueba**
than **que**
thank (verb) **agradecer**; *thank*
  you **gracias**; *thanks* **gracias**
that **ese/esa, eso**;
  that bus **ese autobús**;
  that man **ese hombre**;
  that woman **esa mujer**;
  what's that? **¿qué es eso?**;
  I think that … **creo que …**;
  that one **ése/ésa**
the **el/la**; (plural) **los/las**
theater **el teatro**
their: *their room* **su**
  habitación; *their books* **sus**
  libros; *it's theirs* **es suyo**
them: *it's for them* **es para**
  ellos/ellas; *give*
  it to them **déselo**
then **entonces**;
  (after) **después**
there **allí**; *there is/are …* **hay …**;
  is/are there …? **¿hay …?**
these: *these men* **estos**
  hombres; *these women*
  estas mujeres; *these are*
  mine **éstos son míos**
they **ellos/ellas**
thick **grueso**
thief **el ladrón**
thin **delgado**
think **pensar**; *I think so*
  creo que sí; *I'll think*
  about it **lo pensaré**
third **tercero**
thirsty: *I'm thirsty* **tengo sed**
thirteen **trece**
thirty **treinta**
this: *this one* **éste/ésta**; *this*
  man **este hombre**; *this*
  woman **esta mujer**; *what's*
  this? **¿qué es esto?**; *this is*
  Mr. … **éste es el señor …**
those: *those men* **esos**
  hombres; *those women*
  esas mujeres
thousand **mil**
throat **la garganta**

through **por**
three **tres**
thumbtack **la chincheta**
thunderstorm **la tormenta**
Thursday **jueves**
ticket (train, etc.) **el billete**;
  (theater, etc.) **la entrada**
ticket office **la taquilla**
tide **la marea**
tie **la corbata**; (verb) **atar**
tight **ajustado**
time **tiempo**; *what's the time?*
  ¿qué hora es?
tin **la hojalata**
tip (end) **la punta**;
  (money) **la propina**
tire **el neumático**
tired **cansado**
tire iron **la llave**
  de las tuercas
tissues **los pañuelos**
  de papel
to: *to America* **a América**; *to*
  the station **a la estación**;
  to the doctor **al médico**
toast **la tostada**
tobacco **el tabaco**
tobacconist **el estanco**
today **hoy**
together **juntos**
toilet **el váter**
toilet paper
  el papel higiénico
tomato **el tomate**
tomato juice **el zumo**
  de tomate
tomorrow **mañana**
tongue **la lengua**
tonic **la tónica**
tonight **esta noche**
too (also) **también**;
  (excessively) **demasiado**
tooth **el diente**; *back tooth*
  la muela
toothache **el dolor**
  de muelas
toothbrush **el cepillo**
  de dientes
toothpaste **la pasta dentífrica**
tour **la excursión**
tourist **el/la turista**
tourist office **la oficina**
  de turismo
towel **la toalla**
tower **la torre**
town **el pueblo**
town hall **el ayuntamiento**
toy **el juguete**
trade fair **la feria**
tractor **el tractor**
traffic **el tráfico**

traffic jam **el atasco**
traffic lights **el semáforo**
trailer **la caravana,**
  el remolque
train **el tren**
trainee **el aprendiz**
translate **traducir**
translator **el traductor/**
  la traductora
trash can **el contendor**
  de basura, el cubo
  de la basura
travel agency **la agencia**
  de viajes
tray **la bandeja**
tree **el árbol**
truck **el camión**
trunk (car) **el maletero**
true **cierto**; *it's true* **es verdad**
try **intentar**
Tuesday **martes**
tunnel **el túnel**
turn (left/right) **tuerza** (a la
  izquierda/ a la derecha)
turn: *it's my turn* **me toca**
  a mí
turn signal **el intermitente**
tweezers **las pinzas**
twelve **doce**
twenty **veinte**
two **dos**
typewriter **la máquina**
  de escribir

U

ugly **feo**
umbrella **el paraguas**
uncle **el tío**
under … **debajo de …**
underpants **los calzoncillos**
understand **entender**; *I don't*
  understand **no entiendo**
underwear **la ropa interior**
United States
  Estados Unidos
university **la universidad**
unleaded **sin plomo**
until **hasta**
unusual **poco común**
up **arriba**; *(upward)*
  hacia arriba
urgent **urgente**
us: *it's for us* **es para**
  nosotros/nosotras;
  give it to us **dénoslo**
use **el uso**; (verb) **usar**; *it's no*
  use **no sirve de nada**
useful **útil**
usual **corriente**
usually **en general**

V

vacancies (rooms)
  habitaciones libres
vacation **las vacaciones**
vaccination **la vacuna**
vacuum cleaner **la aspiradora**
valley **el valle**
valve **la válvula**
vanilla **la vainilla**
vase **el jarrón**
veal **la** (carne de) **ternera**
vegetables **la verdura**
vegetarian **vegetariano**
vehicle **el vehículo**
very **muy;** very much **mucho**
vest **la camiseta**
vet **el veterinario**
video (tape) **la cinta
  de vídeo;** (film) **el vídeo**
video games **los vídeo-juegos**
video recorder
  el (aparato de) **vídeo**
view **la vista**
viewfinder **el visor de imagen**
villa **el chalet**
village **el pueblo**
vinegar **el vinagre**
violin **el violín**
visit **la visita; visitar** (verb)
visiting hours **las horas
  de visita**
visitor **el/la visitante**
vitamin pills **las vitaminas**
vodka **el vodka**
voice **la voz**
voicemail **la mensajería
  de voz**

W

wait **esperar;** wait! **¡espere!**
waiter **el camarero;**
  waiter! **¡camarero!**
waiting room **la sala
  de espera**
waitress **la camarera;**
  waitress! **¡Oiga, por favor!**
Wales **Gales**
walk (stroll) **el paseo;** (verb)
  andar; to go for a walk
  ir de paseo
wall **la pared;** (outside)
  el muro
wallet **la cartera**
want (verb) **querer**
war **la guerra**
wardrobe **el armario**
warm **caliente;**
  (weather) **caluroso**

was **estaba/era**
washing machine **la zapatilla**
wasp **la avispa**
watch **el reloj;** (verb) **mirar**
water **el agua**
waterfall **la cascada**
water heater
  el calentador (de agua)
wave **la ola;** (verb) **agitar**
wavy (hair) **ondulado**
we **nosotros/nosotras**
weather **el tiempo**
website **la web site,
  el sitio web**
wedding **la boda**
Wednesday **miércoles**
weeds **las malas hierbas**
week **la semana**
welcome (adj) **bienvenido;**
  (verb) **dar la bienvenida;**
  you're welcome
  no hay de qué
wellington boots
  las botas de agua
Welsh **galés/galesa**
were: you were (informal
  singular) **eras/estabas;**
  (formal singular) **era/
  estaba;** (informal plural)
  erais/estabais; (formal
  plural) **eran/estaban;**
  we were **éramos/
  estábamos;** they were
  eran/estaban
west **el oeste**
wet **mojado**
what? **¿qué?**
wheel **la rueda**
wheelchair **la silla de ruedas**
when? **¿cuándo?**
where? **¿dónde?**
whether **si**
which? **¿cuál?**
whiskey **el whisky**
white **blanco**
who? **¿quién?**
why? **¿por qué?**
wide **ancho;** 3 meters wide
  **de tres metros
  de anchura**
wife **la mujer**
wind **el viento**
window **la ventana**
windshield **el parabrisas**
wine **el vino**
wine list **la carta de
  vinos**
wine merchant **el vinatero**
wing **el ala**
with **con**

without **sin**
witness **el testigo**
woman **la mujer**
wood (material) **la madera**
wool **la lana**
word **la palabra**
work **el trabajo;** (verb)
  trabajar; (to function)
  funcionar
worse **peor**
worst **(el) peor**
wrapping paper
  el papel de envolver;
  (for presents) **el papel
  de regalo**
wrench **la llave inglesa**
wrist **la muñeca**
writing paper **el papel
  de escribir**
wrong **equivocado**

X, Y, Z

X-ray department **el servicio
  de radiología**
year **el año**
yellow **amarillo**
yes **sí**
yesterday **ayer**
yet **todavía;** not yet
  todavía no
yogurt **el yogur**
you (informal singular)
  tú; (formal singular)
  usted; (informal plural, m/f)
  vosotros/vosotras;
  (formal plural) **ustedes**
young **joven**
your: your book (informal
  singular) **tu libro;** (formal
  singular) **su libro;** your
  shoes (informal singular)
  tus zapatos; (formal
  singular) **sus zapato**
yours: is this yours? (informal)
  ¿es tuyo esto?; (formal)
  ¿es suyo esto?
youth hostel
  el albergue juvenil
ZIP code **el código
  postalzipper la
  cremallera**
zoo **el zoo**

DICTIONARY
Spanish to English

The gender of Spanish nouns listed here is indicated by the abbreviations (m) and (f) for masculine and feminine. Plural nouns are followed by the abbreviations (m pl) or (f pl). Spanish adjectives (adj) vary according to the gender and number of the word they describe, and the masculine form is shown here. In general, adjectives that end in **-o** adopt an **-a** ending in the feminine form, and those that end in **-e** usually stay the same. For the plural form, an **-s** is added.

A

a to; **a América** to America; **a la estación** to the station; **al médico** to the doctor; **a las tres** at 3 o'clock
abanico (m) fan (handheld)
abierto open (adj)
abogado/abogada (m/f) lawyer
abrebotellas (m) bottle opener
abrelatas (m) can opener
abrigo (m) coat
abril April
abrir to open
abuela (f) grandmother
abuelo (m) grandfather
abuelos (m pl) grandparents
aburrido boring
acaba de llegar it's just arrived
accidente (m) accident
aceite (m) oil; **el aceite de oliva** olive oil
aceituna (f) olive
acelerador (m) accelerator
acera (f) pavement
acondicionador (m) conditioner (hair)
acuerdo: me acuerdo I remember; **no me acuerdo** I don't remember
adaptador (m) adapter
adelantar pass (car)
adiós goodbye
aduana (f) customs
aerodeslizador (m) hovercraft
aeropuerto (m) airport
afeitado (m) shave; **afeitarse** to shave
after-shave (m) aftershave
afueras (f pl) suburbs
agencia (f) agency

agencia de viajes (f) travel agency
agenda (f) planner
agitar to wave
agosto August
agradable pleasant
agradecer to thank
agua (m) water; **el agua con gas** sparkling water; **el agua mineral** mineral water; **el agua potable** drinking water; **el agua sin gas** still water
aguja (f) needle
ahora now; **¿y ahora qué?** what next?
aire (m) air
aire acondicionado (m) air conditioning
ajedrez (m) chess
ajo (m) garlic
ajustado tight
ala (m) wing
albañil (m) handyman, builder
albaricoque (m) apricot
albergue juvenil (m) youth hostel
alcachofa (f) artichoke
alcohol (m) alcohol
alegre glad
alemán German
Alemania Germany
alérgico allergic
alfiler (m) pin
alfombra (f) carpet; rug
algo something
algodón (m) cotton, cotton balls
alguien somebody
alguna: en alguna parte somewhere
allí there, over there
almohada (f) pillow
alojamiento (m) accommodation
alquilar to rent

alto high, tall, loud
¡alto! stop!
amante (m/f) lover
amargo bitter
amarillo yellow
ambulancia (f) ambulance
América America
americano/americana (m/f) American
amigo/amiga (m/f) friend; **amigo/amiga por correspondencia** (m/f) pen pal
amontillado medium (sherry)
amor (m) love
ampliación (f) enlargement
ampolla (f) blister
análisis de sangre (m) blood test
andar to walk
andén (m) platform
anfiteatro (m) lecture theater
anfitriona (f) hostess
anillo (m) ring (jewelry)
animal (m) animal; **los animales de compañía/los animales domésticos** pets
año (m) year
antes de ... before ...
anticonceptivo (m) contraceptive
anticongelante (m) antifreeze
anticuario (m) antique shop
antiséptico (m) antiseptic
aparcamiento (m) parking lot
aparcar to park; **prohibido aparacar** no parking
apartamento (m) apartment
apellido (m) surname
aperitivo (m) aperitif
apetito (m) appetite
aprender learn

aprendiz (m) *trainee*
apretón de manos (m)
 handshake
araña (f) *spider*
árbol (m) *tree*
árbol de levas (m) *camshaft*
arcón (m) *chest (furniture)*
arena (f) *sand*
Argelia *Algeria*
armario (m) *cupboard,
 wardrobe*
arreglar *repair*
arriba *up;* hacia arriba
 upward
arroyo (m) *stream (small river)*
arroz (m) *rice*
arte (m) *art*
artículos de punto
 (m pl) *knitwear*
artista (m/f) *artist*
asado *roasted*
ascensor (m) *lift*
asiento (m) *seat;*
 el asiento infantil
 car seat (for a baby/child)
asistenta (f) *cleaner*
asmático *asthmatic*
aspiradora (f) *vacuum
 cleaner*
aspirina (f) *aspirin*
atar *to tie*
atasco (m) *traffic jam*
aterrizar *to land*
ático (m) *attic*
atractivo *attractive (offer)*
audífono (m) *hearing aid*
auriculares (m pl)
 headphones
Australia *Australia*
australiano/australiana
 (m/f) *Australian*
autobús (m) *bus;*
 autobús del aeropuerto
 airport bus
autocaravana (f) *camper van*
automático *automatic*
autónomo/autónoma
 (m/f) *self-employed*
autopista (f) *expressway*
avería (f) *(car) breakdown;*
 he tenido una avería
 I've had a breakdown
aves (f pl) *poultry*
avión (m) *aircraft*
avispa (f) *wasp*
ayer *yesterday*
ayuda (f) *help*
ayudar *to help*
ayuntamiento (m) *town hall*
azúcar (m) *sugar*
azul *blue*

B

bacon (m) *bacon*
bailar *to dance*
baile (m) *dance*
bajarse *get off (bus,
 etc.); to get out*
bajo *low, short*
balandro (m) *sailboat*
balcón (m) *balcony*
Baleares: las (Islas)
 Baleares *Balearic Islands*
balón (m) *soccer (ball);*
 el balón de playa
 beach ball
baloncesto (m) *basketball*
bañador (m) *swimsuit,
 swimming trunks*
banco (m) *bank*
banda (f) *band (musicians)*
bandeja (f) *tray*
bandera (f) *flag*
baño (m) *bathtub, bathroom;*
 darse un baño *to take a
 bath;* el traje de baño
 swimsuit
bar (m) *bar (drinks)*
baraja (f) *deck of cards*
barato *inexpensive*
barba (f) *beard*
barbacoa (f) *barbecue*
barca (f) *small boat;*
 la barca de remos
 rowing boat
barco (m) *boat, ship*
barra de labios (f) *lipstick*
bastante *enough,
 quite, fairly*
basura (f) *litter, garbage*
batería (f) *battery (car)*
bebé (m) *baby*
beber *to drink;* ¿quiere
 beber algo? *would
 you like something
 to drink?*
bebida (f) *drink*
beige *beige*
beneficios (m pl) *profits*
berenjenas (f pl)
 eggplant
biblioteca (f) *library*
bicicleta (f) *bicycle;* la
 bicicleta de montaña
 mountain bike
bien *good;* te sienta
 bien *it suits you*
bienvenido *welcome*
bigote (m) *mustache*
billete (m) *fare, ticket (train,
 etc.);* billete de ida y
 vuelta (m) *round-trip ticket*

billete de banco (m)
 banknote
bizcocho (m) *sponge cake*
blanco *white*
blando *soft*
bloc (m) *notepad*
bloque de oficinas (m)
 office block
blusa (f) *blouse*
boca (f) *mouth*
bocadillo (m) *sandwich*
boda (f) *wedding*
bodega (f) *basement*
bolígrafo (m) *ballpoint pen*
bollo (m) *roll (bread)*
bolsa (f) *bag, packet (candy,
 chips);* la bolsa de basura
 garbage bag; la bolsa de
 plástico *plastic bag*
bolsillo (m) *pocket*
bolso (m) *handbag*
bombilla (f) *light bulb*
bonito *nice, pretty,
 attractive (object)*
bordado (m) *embroidery*
borde (m) *edge, border, side*
borracho *drunk*
bosque (m) *forest*
bota (f) *boot*
botas de agua (f pl)
 wellington boots
botella (f) *bottle*
botón (m) *button*
brazo (m) *arm*
bridge (m) *bridge (game)*
británico/británica
 (m/f) *British*
brocha (f) *paint brush*
broche (m) *brooch*
broma (f) *joke*
bronceado *suntanned*
broncearse *suntan: to get
 a suntan*
buenas noches *good evening*
buenas tardes *good
 afternoon*
bueno *good, good to eat, tasty*
buenos días *good morning*
bufanda (f) *scarf*
buzón (m) *mailbox*

C

cabeza (f) *head*
cabina telefónica (f) *phone
 booth*
cable alargador (m)
 extension cord
cacahuetes (m pl) *peanuts*
cada *every, each;* viente euros
 cada uno *20 euros each*

café (m) *café, coffee;*
el café con leche
coffee with milk; **el café**
instantáneo *instant coffee;*
el café solo *espresso*
caja (f) *box; checkout;* **la caja**
de bombones *box of*
chocolates; **la caja de**
cambios *gearbox*
cajero (m) *cashier;*
el cajero automático
ATM
cajetilla (f) *packet (cigarettes)*
calambre (m) *cramp*
calcetines (m pl) *socks*
calculadora (m) *calculator*
calefacción (f) *heating;*
la calefacción central
central heating
calentador (de agua) (m)
water heater
calidad (f) *quality*
caliente *warm*
callado *quiet (person)*
calle (f) *street;* **la calle**
principal main road
caluroso *warm (weather)*
calzoncillos (m pl) *underpants*
cama (f) *bed*
cámara de fotos (f) *camera*
cámara neumática (f)
inner tube
camarera (f) *waitress*
camarero (m) *waiter;*
¡camarero! *waiter!*
cambiar *to change (money)*
cambiarse *to change (clothes)*
cambio (m) *change (money);*
exchange rate
camino (m) *path*
camión (m) *truck*
camisa (f) *shirt*
camiseta (f) *vest*
camisón (m) *nightgown*
campana (f) *bell (church)*
camping (m) *campground*
camping-gas (m) *stove fuel*
campo (m) *countryside, field*
Canadá *Canada*
canadiense *Canadian*
canal (m) *canal*
Canarias: las (Islas)
Canarias Canaries
canción (f) *song*
candado (m) *padlock*
cangrejo (m) *crab*
cansado *tired*
cantar *to sing*
capazo (m) *crib*
capó (m) *hood (car)*
cara (f) *face*

caramelos (m) *candy*
caravana (f) *trailer*
carburador (m) *carburetor*
cardenal (m) *bruise*
cargador (m) *charger*
carne (f) *meat*
carne de cerdo (f) *pork*
carne de vaca (f) *beef*
carnet de conducir (m)
driver's license
carnicería (f) *butcher shop*
caro *expensive*
carpintero (m) *carpenter*
carretera (f) *road*
carrito (m) *cart*
carta (f) *letter (mail); menu;* **la**
carta de vinos (f) *wine list*
cartera (f) *purse, briefcase,*
wallet
carterista (m) *pickpocket*
cartero (m) *mail carrier*
casa (f) *house, home;*
en casa *at home*
casado *married*
cascada (f) *waterfall*
casi *almost*
cassette (f) *cassette*
castaño *brown (hair)*
castañuelas (f pl) *castanets*
castellano *Castilian*
Castilla *Castile*
castillo (m) *castle*
Cataluña *Catalonia*
catedral (f) *cathedral*
catedrático (m) *professor*
católico *Catholic (adj)*
catorce *fourteen*
cazo (m) *saucepan*
cebo (m) *bait*
cebolla (f) *onion*
ceja (f) *eyebrow*
cementerio (m) *cemetery*
cena (f) *dinner, supper,*
dinner party
cenicero (m) *ashtray*
centro (m) *center; downtown;*
el centro deportivo
gym; **en el centro** *middle:*
in the middle
cepillar el pelo *to brush hair*
cepillo (m) *brush (for cleaning);*
el cepillo del pelo hair
brush; **el cepillo de**
dientes *toothbrush*
cerca *near, close;* (f) *fence*
cereza (f) *cherry*
cerilla (f) *match (light)*
cerrado *closed*
cerrar *to close*
cerrojo (m) *bolt (on door)*
certificado (m) *certificate*

cerveza (f) *beer*
césped (m) *lawn*
cesto (m) *basket*
chal (m) *shawl*
chalet (m) *villa*
champiñones (m pl)
mushrooms
champú (m) *shampoo*
chandal (m) *jogging suit*
chaparrón (m) *shower*
(rain)
chaqueta (f) *jacket*
charcutería (f) *delicatessen*
charla (f) *talk*
cheque (m) *check*
chica (f) *girl*
chicle (m) *chewing gum*
chico (m) *boy*
chimenea (f) *chimney,*
fireplace
chincheta (f) *drawing pin*
chiste (m) *joke (funny story)*
chocolate (m) *chocolate*
chuleta (f) *chop (food)*
chupa-chups (m pl) *lollipop*
ciclismo (m) *cycling*
ciclomotor (m) *moped*
ciego *blind (cannot see)*
cielo (m) *sky*
cien *hundred*
ciencias (f pl) *science*
cierto *true*
cigalas (f pl) *crayfish*
cigarrillo (m) *cigarette*
cinco *five*
cincuenta *fifty*
cine (m) *movie theater*
cinta (f) *cassette;* **el cinta**
de vídeo *video tape*
cinturón (m) *belt;* **el cinturón**
de seguridad *seat belt*
cita (f) *appointment*
ciudad (f) *city, town;*
el centro ciudad
downtown
claro *clear (water); light*
(adj: not dark)
clase (f) *class; lesson*
clavo (m) *nail (metal)*
claxon (m) *horn (car)*
cliente (m) *client*
cobrador (m) *conductor (bus)*
cobrar *to cash*
cocer *to cook, boil*
cocer al horno *to bake*
coche (m) *car*
coche-cama (m) *sleeper car*
cochecito (m) *baby carriage*
cocina (f) *stove; kitchen*
cocinero/cocinera (m/f) *cook*
coctel (m) *cocktail party*

código code; el código de la circulación highway code; el código postal ZIP code

codo (m) elbow

coger catch; coger el tren to catch the train

cojín (m) cushion

col (f) cabbage

cola (f) line

colada (f) laundry (washed)

colcha (f) bedspread

colchón (m) mattress

colchoneta (f) air mattress

colección (f) collection (stamps, etc.)

coliflor (f) cauliflower

collar (m) collar (of animal)

collar (m) necklace; color

combinacíon (f) slip (underwear)

comedor (m) dining room

comer to eat

comida (f) food, meal; lunch

comida ligera (f) snack

comisaría (f) police station

como like; como éste like this one

¿cómo? how?; ¿cómo se llama usted? what's your name?¿cómo dice? pardon?, what did you say?

cómoda (f) chest of drawers

compañía aérea (f) airline

compartimento (m) compartment

completamente completely

complicado complicated

compra (f) shopping

comprar to buy

comprendo I see

compresas (f pl) sanitary napkins

con with

coñac (m) brandy

concha (f) shell

concierto (m) concert

concurrido crowded

condón (m) condom

conducir to drive

conductor (m) driver

conejo (m) rabbit

conferencia (f) conference; la sala de conferencias conference room

congelador (m) freezer

congelados (m pl) frozen foods

conocer to know (person, place)

conserje (m) porter (hotel)

consulado (m) consulate

contable (m/f) accountant

contendor de basura (m) trash can

contento happy

contestador automático (m) answering machine

contra against

contraseña (f) password

contrato (m) contract

copa (f) glass (for drinking)

corazón (m) heart

corazones (m pl) hearts (cards)

corbata (f) tie

corcho (m) cork

cordero (m) lamb

cordones (de los zapatos) (m pl) (shoe)laces

correa (f) leash

correcto right (correct)

correo (m) mail; el correo certificado registered mail; el correo electrónico email

Correos: (la oficina de) Correos (f) post office

correr to run

corrida de toros (f) bullfight

corriente ordinary; usual

cortadura (f) cut

cortar to chop, cut

cortauñas (m) nail clippers

corte de pelo (m) haircut

cortina (f) curtain

corto short

coser to sew

cosméticos (m pl) cosmetics

costar to cost; ¿cuánto cuesta? what does it cost?

crema (f) cream (lotion)

crema de zapatos (f) shoe polish

cremallera (f) zip

creo que ... I think that ...

crepes (f pl) pancakes

crisis nerviosa (f) nervous breakdown

cristal (m) glass (material)

crucero (m) cruise

cuaderno (m) notebook

cuadrado square (adj)

¿cuál? which?

cualquiera de ellos either of them

¿cuándo? when?

¿cuánto cuesta? what does it cost?, how much is it?

¿cuántos años tiene? how old are you?

cuarenta forty

cuarto (m) quarter, room; (adj) fourth

cuarto de baño (m) bathroom

cuarto de estar (m) living room, lounge

cuatro four

cubo (m) bucket; el cubo de la basura trash can

cucaracha (f) cockroach

cuchara (f) spoon

cuchillas de afeitar (f pl) razor blades

cuchillo (m) knife

cuello (m) neck, collar

cuenco (m) bowl

cuenta (f) bill

cuerda (f) string; rope

cuerno (m) horn (animal)

cuero (m) leather

cuerpo (m) body

cueva (f) cave

¡cuidado! be careful!

cumpleaños (m) birthday

cuna (f) crib

cura (m) priest

curry (m) curry

D

dar give; dar la bienvenida to welcome

de of; de algún modo somehow; de ida single (ticket)

debajo de below, under

decir say; ¿qué ha dicho? what did you say?; ¿cómo se dice ...? how do you say ...?

declaración (f) statement

dedo (m) finger

delante de in front of ...

delgado thin

demasiado too (excessively)

démelo give it to me

dentadura postiza (f) dentures, false teeth

dentista (m/f) dentist

denuncia (f) police report

departamento (m) department

deporte (m) sports

derecho (m) law, justice; no hay derecho it's not fair; (adj) right (not left)

desayuno (m) breakfast

descansar to rest

descuento (m) discount

desmayarse to faint

desodorante (m) deodorant

despacho (m) office (room)

despegue (m) take off

despertador (m) alarm clock

después then (after);

después de ... after ...

destornillador (m) screwdriver

detergente (m) laundry detergent

detrás de ... behind ...

devolver to return (give back); to be sick (vomit)
día (m) day; **el día de fiesta** public holiday
diabético diabetic
diamantes (m pl) diamonds
diarrea (f) diarrhea
diccionario (m) dictionary
diciembre December
diecinueve nineteen
dieciocho eighteen
dieciséis sixteen
diecisiete seventeen
diente (m) tooth
diesel diesel (adj: engine)
diez ten
diferente different
difícil difficult
dígame hello (on phone)
dinero (m) money, cash; **no tengo dinero** I have no money
dirección (f) address
director/directora (m/f) manager (hotel); conductor (orchestra)
disco (m) record (music)
disco compacto (m) CD
discoteca (f) nightclub
diseñador/diseñadora (m/f) designer
disponible available
distancia distance; **¿qué distancia hay a ...?** how far is it to ...?
distinto separate, different (adj); **¡eso es distinto!** that's different!; **quería otro distinto** I'd like a different one
diversiones (f pl) entertainment
divertido; (odd) raro funny
divorciado divorced
doce twelve
documento (m) document
dólar (m) dollar
dolor (m) ache, pain; **el dolor de cabeza** headache; **el dolor de estómago** stomach-ache; **el dolor de muelas** toothache
domingo Sunday
¿dónde? where?; **¿dónde está ...?** where is ...?
dónut (m) doughnut
dormir to sleep
dormitorio (m) bedroom
dos two; **los dos** both
ducha (f) shower (bath)
dulce sweet (adj: not sour)

dunas (f pl) sand dunes
durante during
duro hard (not soft)
duty-free (m) duty-free shop

E

echar al correo to mail
echar el cerrojo to bolt
edificio (m) building
edredón (m) comforter
eje (m) axle
ejecutivo (m) executive
ejemplo (m) example; **por ejemplo** for example
él he, him, the (m); **es para él** it's for him
elástico elastic
electricidad (f) electricity
electricista (m/f) electrician
eléctrico electric
ella she, her, the (f); **es para ella** it's for her
ellos/ellas they, them; **es para ellos/ellas** it's for them
email (m) email; **la dirección de email** email address
embajada (f) embassy
embarazada pregnant
embarazoso embarrassing
emergencia (f) emergency
empaste (m) filling (in tooth)
empezar to start
empleado (m) employee
empujar to push
en on, at, in; **en inglés** in English; **en el hotel** in the hotel; **en Barcelona** in Barcelona; **en Correos** at the post office; **en su casa** at your place
encaje (m) lace
encantado/encantada (m/f) pleased to meet you
encargado (m) caretaker
encendedor (m) lighter
encendido (m) ignition
enchufe (m) plug (electrical)
encima de ... over ...
encuentro (m) meeting; **no me encuentro bien** I don't feel well
enero January
enfermo/enferma (m/f) nurse
enfrente de across from; **enfrente del hotel** across from the hotel
¡enhorabuena! congratulations!
ensalada (f) salad

entender to understand; **no entiendo** I don't understand
entonces then, so
entrada (f) entrance, ticket (theater, etc.)
entrantes (m pl) starters
entre ... between ...
entrega (f) delivery
enviar por fax to fax
epiléptico epileptic
equipaje (m) luggage; **el equipaje de mano** carry-on luggage
equipo de música (m) music system
equivocación (f) mistake
equivocado wrong
era you were (formal): it/he/she was
éramos we were
eran they were
eras you were (informal)
eres you are (informal)
es you are (formal)
es it/he/she is
escalera (f) staircase; **la escalera mecánica** escalator; **las escaleras** stairs
escarcha (f) frost
escocés/escocesa (m/f) Scottish
Escocia Scotland
escopeta (f) gun (rifle)
escuela (f) school
ese/esa that; **ese autobús** that bus; **ese hombre** that man; **esa mujer** that woman; **¿qué es eso?** what's that?
ése/ésa that, that one;
esmalte de uñas (m) nail polish
esos/esas those, those ones; **esos hombres** those men; **esas mujeres** those women
espalda (f) back (body)
España Spain
español/española (m/f) Spanish, Spaniard
especialidad (f) field of study
espejo (m) mirror
esperar to wait; **¡espere!** wait!
espinacas (f pl) spinach
espuma de afeitar (f) shaving foam
espuma moldeadora (f) mousse (for hair)
esquina (f) corner (of street)

esquís (m pl) *skis*
está *you are* (formal)
está *it/he/she is*
esta noche *tonight*
estaba *it/he/she was; you were* (formal)
estábamos *we were*
estaban *they were*
estabas *you were* (informal)
estaca (f) *tent peg*
estación (f) *station;* la estación de autobuses *bus station;* la estación de esquí *ski resort;* la estación de metro *metro station*
Estados Unidos *United States*
estamos *we are*
están *they are*
estanco (m) *tobacconist*
estaquilla (f) *tent peg*
estás *you are* (informal)
estatua (f) *statue*
este *east;* el Este *the East*
éste/ésta *this, this one;* este hombre *this man;* esta mujer *this woman;* ¿qué es esto? *what's this?;* éste es el señor ... *this is Mr. ...*
estómago (m) *stomach*
estos/estas *these, these ones;* estos hombres *these men;* estas mujeres *these women;* éstos son míos *these are mine*
estoy *I am*
estrecho *narrow* (adj)
estrella (f) *star*
estudiante (m/f) *student*
estufa (f) *heater*
estúpido *stupid*
etiqueta (f) *label*
evidente *clear* (obvious)
excelente *excellent*
exceso de equipaje (m) *excess baggage*
excursión (f) *excursion, tour*
exposición (f) *exhibition*
externa *external*
extintor (m) *fire extinguisher*
extranjero/extranjera (m/f) *foreigner*

F

fácil *easy*
factor de protección (m) *protection factor* (SPF)
factura (f) *invoice*
facturación (f) *check-in*

facturar *to check in*
falda (f) *skirt*
falta: no hace falta *there's no need*
familia (f) *family*
fan (m) *fan* (enthusiast)
fantástico *fantastic*
farmacia (f) *pharmacy*
faros (m pl) *headlights*
febrero *February*
¡felicidades! *happy birthday!*
feliz *happy*
feo *ugly*
feria (f) *fair, trade fair*
ferretería (f) *hardware store*
ferrocarril (m) *railroad*
ferry (m) *ferry*
fiebre (f) *temperature,* fever; la fiebre del heno *hay fever*
fiesta (f) *party* (celebration)
filete (m) *steak*
filtro (m) *filter*
fin (m) *end;* ¡por fin! *at last!*
final (m) *end*
fino *dry* (sherry)
flash (m) *flash* (camera)
flauta (f) *flute*
flequillo (m) *bangs* (hair)
flexo (m) *swing-armlamp*
flor (f) *flower*
folleto (m) *brochure, leaflet*
fonda (f) *inn*
fondo (m) *bottom*
fontanero/fontanera (m/f) *plumber*
foto (grafía) (f) *photograph*
fotocopiadora (f) *photocopier*
fotografiar *to photograph*
fotógrafo (m) *photographer*
fotómetro (m) *light meter*
frambuesa (f) *raspberry*
francés *French*
Francia *France*
fregadero (m) *sink*
freír *to fry*
frenar *to brake*
freno (m) *brake;* el freno de emergencia *emergency brake;* el freno de mano *handbrake*
fresas (f pl) *strawberries*
fresco *cool*
frigorífico (m) *refrigerator*
frío cold (adj); I'm cold tengo frío
frito *fried*
frontera (f) *border* (between countries)
fruta (f) *fruit*

fuego (m) *fire;* los fuegos artificiales *fireworks*
fuel-oil *diesel* (oil)
fuente (f) *fountain*
fuera *outside*
fuerte *strong*
fumar *to smoke*
funcionar *to work* (function)
fútbol (m) *soccer* (game)

G

gabardina (f) *raincoat*
gafas (f pl) *glasses;* las gafas de sol *sunglasses*
galería de arte (f) *art gallery*
Gales *Wales*
galés/galesa *Welsh*
galleta (f) *cookie*
gambas (f pl) *shrimp*
ganga (f) *bargain*
garage (m) *garage* (for parking)
garantía (f) *guarantee*
garantizar *to guarantee*
garganta (f) *throat*
gas para el encendedor (m) *lighter fuel*
gasolina (f) *gasoline*
gasolinera (f) *gas station*
gato (m) *cat*
gay *gay* (homosexual)
gel (m) *gel* (hair); el gel de ducha *shower gel*
gemelos (m pl) *cuff links*
general: en general *usually*
gente (f) *people*
gerente (m/f) *manager*
Gibraltar *Gibraltar*
ginebra (f) *gin*
gobierno (m) *government*
Golfo de Vizcaya (m) *Bay of Biscay*
goma (f) *rubber band; rubber* (material)
goma de borrar (f) *eraser*
gordo *fat* (adj)
gorra (f) *cap* (hat)
gorro (m) *woollen hat*
gotas (f pl) *drops*
gracias *thank you*
Gran Bretaña *Great Britain*
grande *big, large*
grandes almacenes (m pl) *department store*
granja (f) *farm*
granjero (m) *farmer*
grapadora (f) *stapler*
grasa (f) *fat* (meat, etc.)
gratis *free* (no charge)
grifo (m) *faucet*

gris *gray*
gritar *to shout*
grosellas negras (f pl) *black currants*
grueso *thick*
grupo (m) *party (group)*
guantes (m pl) *gloves*
guapo *attractive, beautiful, handsome (person)*
guerra (f) *war*
guía (m/f) *guide;* **la guía telefónica** *phone book;* **la guía turística** *guide book*
guisantes (m pl) *peas*
guisar *to cook*
guitarra (f) *guitar*
gustar *like:* **me gusta ...** *I like ...;* **me gusta nadar** *I like swimming*

H

habitación (f) *room;* **la habitación doble** *double room;* **la habitación individual** *single room;* **habitaciones libres** *vacancies*
hablar *to talk;* **¿habla ...?** *do you speak ...?;* **no hablo ...** *I don't speak ...*
hacer *to do, make;* **hacer auto-stop** *to hitchhike;* **hacer footing** *to jog;* **hacer punto** *to knit;* **hacer transbordo** *to change (trains, etc.);* **hace sol** *it's sunny*
hacha (m) *axe*
hacia abajo *down*
hambre *hungry;* **tengo hambre** *I'm hungry*
hamburguesa (f) *hamburger*
hámster (m) *hamster*
harina (f) *flour*
hasta *until*
hay... *there is/are...;* **¿hay ...?** *is/are there ...?*
helado (m) *ice cream*
hepatitis (f) *hepatitis*
herida (f) *injury*
hermana (f) *sister*
hermano (m) *brother*
hervido *boiled*
hervidor de agua (m) *teakettle*
hervir *to boil (water)*
hidroaleta (f) *hydrofoil*
hielo (m) *ice*
hierba (f) *grass*
hierro (m) *iron (material)*
hígado (m) *liver*

higo (m) *fig*
hija (f) *daughter*
hijastra (f) *stepdaughter*
hijastro (m) *stepson*
hijo (m) *son*
hincha (f) *soccer fan*
historia (f) *history*
hobby (m) *hobby*
hoguera (f) *campfire*
hoja (f) *leaf, sheet (of paper)*
hojalata (f) *tin*
hola *hello*
hombre (m) *man*
hombro (m) *shoulder*
homeopatía (f) *homeopathy*
honrado *honest*
hora (f) *hour;* **¿qué hora es?** *what's the time?*
horario (m) *schedule;* **el horario de apertura** *opening times*
horca (f) *garden fork*
horno (m) *oven*
horrible *awful, horrible*
hospital (m) *hospital*
hoy *today*
hueso (m) *bone*
huevo (m) *egg*
húmedo *damp*
humo (m) *smoke*

I

idioma (m) *language*
iglesia (f) *church*
imperdible (m) *safety pin*
imposible *impossible*
impreso de solicitud (m) *application form*
impresora (f) *printer*
incendio (m) *fire (blaze)*
incluido *included*
indigestión *indigestion*
infección (f) *infection*
información (f) *information*
informe (m) *report*
ingeniería (f) *engineering*
Inglaterra *England*
inglés/inglesa *English*
inhalador (m) *inhaler (for asthma, etc.)*
inmediatamente *immediately*
insecto (m) *insect*
insolación (f) *sunstroke*
insomnio (m) *insomnia*
instrumento musical (m) *musical instrument*
intentar *to try*
interesante *interesting*
intermitente (m) *turn signal*

internet (m) *Internet*
interpretar *to interpret*
intérprete (m/f) *interpreter*
interruptor (m) *switch*
intoxicación alimenticia (f) *food poisoning*
invitación (f) *invitation*
invitada (f) *guest*
inyección (f) *injection*
ir *to go;* **ir a esquiar** *to go skiing;* **ir de compras** *to go shopping*
Irlanda *Ireland;* **Irlanda del Norte** *Northern Ireland*
irlandés/irlandesa *Irish*
isla (f) *island*
Italia *Italy*
italiano/italiana (m/f) *Italian*
izquierdo *left (not right)*

J

jabón (m) *soap;* **el jabón de lavadora** *laundry detergent*
jamón (m) *ham*
jarabe (m) *syrup*
jardín (m) *garden*
jarrita (f) *mug*
jarrón (m) *vase*
jaula (f) *cage*
jazz (m) *jazz*
jefe (m) *manager*
jengibre (m) *ginger (spice)*
jerez (m) *sherry*
jeringuilla (f) *syringe*
jersey (m) *sweater*
joven *young*
joyería (f) *jeweler*
judías (f pl) *beans*
jueves *Thursday*
jugar *to play*
juguete (m) *toy*
julio *July*
junio *June*
junto a *near;* **junto a la puerta** *near the door;* **junto a la ventana** *near the window*
juntos *together*

K, L

kilo (m) *kilo*
kilómetro (m) *kilometer*
kiosko de periódicos (m) *newsstand*
la (f) *the*
laca (f) *hairspray*
lado de (f) *beside*
ladrón (m) *thief*

lago (m) *lake*
lámpara (f) *lamp*
lamparilla de noche (f) *bedside lamp*
lana (f) *wool*
langosta (f) *lobster*
lápiz (m) *pencil*
largo *long*
las (f pl) *the*
lata (f) *can (tin)*
lavabo (m) *basin (sink)*
lavandería automática (f) *laundromat*
lavavajillas (m) *dishwasher*
laxante (m) *laxative*
leche (f) *milk;* **la leche limpiadora** *cleansing milk (for skin)*
lechuga (f) *lettuce*
leer *to read*
lejía *bleach*
lejos *far, far away*
lengua (f) *tongue*
lente (f) *lens;* **las lentes de contacto** *contact lenses;* **las lentes de contacto semi-rígidas** *gas-permeable lenses*
lento *slow*
letra (f) *letter (of alphabet)*
levantarse *to get up (rise)*
libra (f) *pound (sterling)*
libre *free (not engaged)*
libre de impuestos *duty-free*
libro (m) *book;* **el libro de frases** *phrase book*
licor (m) *liqueur*
ligero *light (adj: not heavy)*
lima (f) *lime (fruit)*
lima de uñas (f) *nailfile*
límite de velocidad (m) *speed limit*
limón (m) *lemon*
limonada (f) *lemonade*
limpio *clean (adj)*
línea (f) *line (phone, etc.)*
linterna (f) *flashlight*
listo *clever; ready*
literatura (f) *literature*
litro (m) *liter*
llamar por teléfono *to telephone*
llave (f) *key;* **la llave de las tuercas** *tire iron;* **la llave inglesa** *wrench*
llegar *to arrive*
lleno *crowded, full;* **estoy lleno** *I'm full*
llorar *to cry (weep)*
lluvia (f) *rain*
lo/la *it*

lo antes posible *as soon as possible*
loción *lotion* (f); **la loción anti-mosquitos** *insect repellent lotion;* **la loción bronceadora** *suntan lotion*
loco *crazy*
lona impermeable (f) *groundsheet*
longitud (f) *length*
los (m pl) *the*
lo siento *I'm sorry*
luces de posición (f pl) *side lights*
lugar (m) *place, sight;* **los lugares de interés de ...** *the sights of ...*
luna (f) *moon*
lunes *Monday*
luz (f) *light*

M

madastra (f) *stepmother*
madera (f) *wood (material)*
madre (f) *mother*
maduro *ripe*
malas hierbas (f pl) *weeds*
maleta (f) *suitcase*
maletero (m) *trunk (car)*
Mallorca *Majorca*
malo *bad, poor (quality)*
mama *Mum*
mañana *tomorrow*
mañana (f) *morning;* **por la mañana** *in the morning*
mandar *to send*
mandarina (f) *tangerine*
manga (f) *sleeve*
mano (f) *hand*
manta (f) *blanket, rug*
mantequilla (f) *butter*
manzana (f) *apple*
mapa (m) *map*
maquillaje (m) *make-up*
maquina cortacésped (f) *lawn mower*
máquina de escribir (f) *typewriter*
máquina de fotos (f) *camera*
mar (m) *sea*
marea (f) *tide*
mareado *faint, dizzy*
margarina (f) *margarine*
marido (m) *husband*
mariscos (m pl) *seafood, shellfish*
mármol (m) *marble*
marrón *brown*
Marruecos *Morocco*
martes *Tuesday*

martillo (m) *hammer*
marzo *March*
más *more;* **más de ...** *more than ...;* **más tarde** *later;* **algo más** *something else;* **alguien más** *someone else*
mástil (m) *tent pole*
matrícula (f) *license plate*
mayo *may*
mecánico (m) *mechanic*
media pensión *half board*
medianoche *midnight*
medias (f pl) *pantyhose, stockings*
medicina (f) *medicine*
médico/médica (m/f) *doctor*
medio *half;* **media hora** *half an hour*
mediodía (m) *noon*
Mediterráneo: el Mediterráneo *Mediterranean*
medusa (f) *jellyfish*
mejillones (m pl) *mussels*
mejor *best/better*
melocotón (m) *peach*
melón (m) *melon*
menos *less*
mensaje (m) *message*
mensajería de voz (f) *voicemail*
menú (del día) (m) *set menu*
menudo: a menudo *often*
mercado (m) *market*
mermelada (f) *jam;* **la mermelada de naranja** *marmalade*
mes (m) *month*
mesa (f) *table;* **la mesa de escritorio** *desk*
mesilla de noche (f) *nightstand*
metro (m) *subway*
mi (s) *my;* **mi libro** *my book;* **mis llaves** *my keys*
microondas (m) *microwave*
miel (f) *honey*
miércoles *Wednesday*
mil *thousand*
minusválido *disabled*
minuto (m) *minute*
mío *mine;* **es mío** *it's mine*
mirar *to watch*
misa (f) *mass (church)*
mismo *same;* **el mismo vestido** *the same dress;* **la misma gente** *the same people;* **lo mismo otra vez, por favor** *same again, please*
mochila (f) *backpack*

moda (f) *fashion*
modem (m) *modem*
mojado *wet*
moneda (f) *coin*
monedero (m) *purse*
monitor (m) *monitor*
montaña (f) *mountain*
monte (m) *hill*
monumento (m)
monument
morado *purple*
moras (f pl) *blackberries*
mordedura (f) *bite* (dog)
morder *to bite* (dog)
morir *to die*
mosaico (m) *mosaic*
mosca (f) *fly* (insect)
mosquito (m) *mosquito*
mostaza (f) *mustard*
mostrador (m) *countertop*; **el mostrador de facturación** *check-in desk*
motocicleta (f) *motorcycle*
motor (m) *engine* (motor)
motora (f) *motorboat*
mover *to move* (something); **moverse** *move oneself*; **¡no se mueva!** *don't move!*
mucho *much/many, a lot*; **mucho mejor** *much better*; **mucho más despacio** *much slower*; **no muchos** *not many*
mudarse (de casa) *to move* (house)
muebles (m pl) *furniture*
muela (f) *back tooth*
muelle (m) *dock*; *spring* (mechanical)
muerto *dead*
mujer (f) *woman, wife*
muletas (f pl) *crutches*
muñeca (f) *wrist*
muro (m) *wall* (outside)
museo (m) *museum*
música (f) *music*; **la música clásica** *classical music*; **la música folklórica** *folk music*; **la música pop** *pop music*
músico (m) *musician*
muy *very*

N

nací en ... *I was born in ...*
nada *nothing*; **no queda nada** *there's nothing left*; **no sirve de nada** *it's no use*
nadar *to swim*
nadie *nobody*

naranja (f) *orange* (fruit); *orange* (adj)
nariz (f) *nose*
nata (f) *cream* (dairy)
natación (f) *swimming*
náuseas *sick*; **tengo náuseas** *I feel sick*
navaja (f) *penknife*
navidad (f) *Christmas*
necesario *necessary*
necesito ... *I need ...*
negar *to deny*
negativo (m) *negative* (photo)
negocio (m) *business*
negro *black*
neozelandés/ neozelandesa *New Zealander*
neumático (m) *tire*
ni ... ni ... *neither ... nor ...*
niebla (f) *fog*
nieta (f) *granddaughter*
nieto (m) *grandson*
nieve (f) *snow*
ninguno/ninguna: ninguno de ellos *neither of them*; **en ninguna parte** *nowhere*
niño/niña *child* (m/f); **los niños** *children*; **el niño pequeño** *baby*
no *no* (response), *not*; **no hay de qué** *you're welcome*; **no importa** *it doesn't matter*; **no es/está ...** *(s)he's not ...*
noche (f) *night*
nombre (m) *name*; **el nombre de pila** *first name*
norte (m) *north*
nosotros/nosotras *we, us*; **es para nosotros/ nosotras** *it's for us*
noticias (f pl) *news*
novela (f) *novel*
noventa *ninety*
novia (f) *girlfriend*
noviembre *November*
novio (m) *boyfriend*
nudista (m/f) *nudist*
nuestro *our*; **es nuestro** *it's ours*
Nueva Zelanda *New Zealand*
nueve *nine*
nuevo *new*
nuez (f) *nut* (fruit)
número (m) *number*; **los números** *figures*
nunca *never*

O

o *or*; **o bien ... o ...** *either ... or ...*
obra de teatro (f) *play* (theater)
obturador (m) *shutter* (camera)
Océano Atlántico (m) *Atlantic Ocean*
ochenta *eighty*
ocho *eight*
octubre *October*
oculista (m/f) *optician*
ocupado *busy* (phone); *occupied*
oeste (m) *west*
oficina (f) *office* (place); *branch* (of company); **la oficina de objetos perdidos** *lost property office*; **la oficina de turismo** *tourist office*
oído (m) (inner) *ear*
¡oiga, por favor! *excuse me!* (to get attention); *waiter/waitress!*
oír *to hear*
ojo (m) *eye*
ola (f) *wave*
oler *to smell*
olivo (m) *olive tree*
olor (m) *smell*
oloroso *sweet* (sherry)
olvidar *to forget*
once *eleven*
ondulado *wavy* (hair)
operación (f) *operation*
operadora (f) *operator*
oporto (m) *port* (drink)
orden del día (m) *agenda*
ordenador (m) *computer*
oreja *ear* (f)
órgano (m) *organ* (music)
oro (m) *gold*
orquesta (f) *orchestra*
oscuro *dark*; **azul oscuro** *dark blue*
ostra (f) *oyster*
otra vez *again*
otro *another; other*; **el otro** *the other one*; **en otro sitio** *somewhere else*

P

padastro (m) *stepfather*
padre (m) *father*; **los padres** *parents*
pagar *to pay*; **pagar al contado** *to pay cash*

página (f) *page*
pago (m) *payment*
país (m) *country* (state)
pájaro (m) *bird*
pala (f) *spade*
palabra (f) *word*
palacio (m) *palace*
palanca de velocidades (f)
gear stick
pálido *pale*
pan (m) *bread*
panadería (f) *bread shop*
pañal (m) *diaper*;
los pañales desechables
disposable diapers
paño de cocina (m)
dish cloth
pantalla (f) *lampshade, screen*
pantalón (m) *pants, trousers*;
los pantalones cortos
shorts
pantis (m pl) *pantyhose*
pañuelo (m) *headscarf*; **los**
pañuelos de papel *tissues*
papá *dad*
papel (m) *paper*;
el papel de envolver/
regalo *wrapping paper*; **el**
papel de escribir *writing*
paper; **el papel higiénico**
toilet paper; **los papeles de**
filtro *filter papers*
paquete (m)
package, packet, parcel
par (m) *pair*
para *for*; **es para mí** *it's for*
me; **para el viernes** *by*
Friday; **¿para qué?** *what*
for?; **para una semana**
for a week
parabrisas (m) *windshield*
parachoques (m) *bumper*
parada (f) *stop* (bus); **la**
parada de taxis *taxi stand*
parafina (f) *kerosene*
paraguas (m) *umbrella*
parar *to stop*
pared (f) *wall* (inside)
pariente (m) *relative*
parque (m) *park*
parrilla (f) *grill*
parte de atrás (f)
back (not front)
parterre (m) *flowerbed*
partido (m) *match* (sports);
party (political)
pasajero (m) *passenger*
pasaporte (m) *passport*;
el pasaporte de
animales *pet passport*
pasas (f pl) *raisins*

paseo (m) *walk, stroll*; **ir de**
paseo *to go for a walk*
pasillo (m) *aisle, corridor*
paso elevado (m) *overpass*
pasta (f) *pasta*
pasta dentífrica (f) *toothpaste*
pastel (m) *cake* (small)
pastelería (f) *bakery*
pastilla (f) *pill, tablet*; **las**
pastillas de menta
peppermints; **las pastillas**
para la garganta
cough drops
patata (f) *potato*; **las patatas**
fritas *french fries, chips*
patinar *to skid*
patines para hielo (m pl)
ice skates
peatón (m) *pedestrian*
pecho (m) *chest* (part of body)
pedazo (m) *piece*
pedido (m) *order*
pegamento (m) *adhesive, glue*
peinar *to comb*
peine (m) *comb*
película (f) *film, movie*; **la**
película en color *color film*
peligroso *dangerous*
pelo (m) *hair*
pelota (f) *ball*
peluquería (f) *hairdresser*;
la peluquería de
caballeros *barber*
pendientes (m pl) *earrings*
pensar *to think*; **lo pensaré**
I'll think about it
pensión completa *full board*
peor *worse, worst*
pepino (m) *cucumber*
pequeño *little, small*
pera (f) *pear*
percha (f) *coat hanger*
¡perdón! *sorry!, excuse me!*
(when sneezing, etc.)
perejil (m) *parsley*
perezoso *lazy*
perfecto *perfect*
perfume (m) *perfume*
periódico (m) *newspaper*
perla (f) *pearl*
permanente (f) *perm*
permiso (m) *license*
pero *but*
perro (m) *dog*
persianas (f pl) *blinds*
pesado *heavy*
pesca (f) *fishing*
pescadería (f) *fishmonger*
pescado (m) *fish* (food)
pescar: ir a pescar
to go fishing

pez (m) *fish* (animal)
piano (m) *piano*
picadura (f) *bite* (by insect)
picaporte (m) *handle* (door)
picar *to bite* (insect)
picas (f pl) *spades* (cards)
picnic (m) *picnic*
pie (m) *foot*
pierna (f) *leg*
pijama (m) *pajamas*
pila (f) *battery* (flashlight, etc.)
piloto (m) *pilot*
pimienta (f) *pepper* (spice)
pimiento (m)
pepper (red, green)
pin (m) *PIN*
piña (f) *pineapple*
pinchazo (m) *puncture*
pino (m) *pine* (tree)
pintor (m) *decorator*
pintura (f) *paint*
pinza (f) *peg*;
las pinzas *tweezers*
pipa (f) *pipe* (for smoking)
Pirineos: los Pirineos
Pyrenees
piscina (f) *swimming pool*;
la piscina municipal *public*
swimming pool
piso (m)
apartment; *floor* (story)
pista (f) *runway*
pistola (f) *gun* (pistol)
piston (m) *piston*
pizza (f) *pizza*
plancha (f) *iron* (for clothes);
a la plancha *grilled*
planchar *to iron*
plano (m) *town map, town*
plan; (adj) *flat, level*
planta (f) *plant*
planta baja (f) *ground floor*
plástico (m) *plastic*;
el plástico para envolver
plastic wrap
plata (f) *silver* (metal)
plátano (m) *banana*
plateado *silver* (color)
platillo (m) *saucer*
plato (m) *plate*; **el plato**
principal *main course*;
los platos preparados
prepared meals
playa (f) *beach*
plaza (f) *site, square*
(in town); **la plaza de**
toros *bullring*
pluma (f) *pen*;
la pluma estilográfica
fountain pen
pobre *poor* (not rich)

poco *a little;* **poco común** *unusual;* **poco hecho/ pasado** *rare (steak)*
poder *to be able*
policía (f) *police*
policía (m) *police officer*
política (f) *politics*
pollo (m) *chicken*
polvo (m) *powder;* **los polvos** *make-up powder;* **los polvos de talco** *talcum powder*
pomada (f) *ointment*
poner *to put;* **¿me pone ...?** *can I have ...?*
poquito *a little;* **sólo un poquito** *just a little*
por *through, by, per;* **por avión** *by air mail;* **por la noche** *at night;* **por noche** *per night;* **por todas partes** *everywhere*
porcelana (f) *china(wear)*
por favor *please*
¿por qué? *why?*
porque *because*
portero (m) *caretaker*
Portugal *Portugal*
portugués *Portuguese*
posible *possible*
postal (f) *postcard*
póster (m) *poster*
postigo (m) *shutter (window)*
postre (m) *dessert*
precio (m) *price;* **el precio de entrada** (m) *admission charge*
precioso *beautiful (object)*
preferir *to prefer*
pregunta (f) *question*
presupuesto (m) *budget, estimate*
primavera (f) *spring (season)*
primer piso (m) *first floor*
primero *first;* **de primera** *first class;* **primeros auxilios** *first aid*
primo (m) *cousin*
prima (f) *cousin*
principiante (m/f) *beginner*
principio (m) *start, beginning*
prisa: tengo prisa *I'm in a hurry*
privado *private*
problema (m) *problem*
producto (m) *product;* **los productos de belleza** *beauty products;* **los productos del hogar** *household products;* **los productos lácteos** *dairy products*

profesión (f) *profession*
profesor/profesora (m/f) *teacher*
profesor/profesora de universidad (m/f) *professor (university)*
profundo *deep*
programa (m) *schedule*
prohibido *prohibited*
prometida (f) *fiancée*
prometido (m) *fiancé*
prometido/prometida (m/f) *engaged (to be married)*
propina (f) *tip (money)*
próximo *next*
prudente *careful*
prueba (f) *test*
público *public*
pueblo (m) *small town, village*
¿puede ...? *can you ...?*
puedo *I can;* **no puedo** *I can't*
puente (m) *bridge*
puerta (f) *door, gate;* **la puerta de embarque** *departure gate*
puerto (m) *harbor, port*
pulga (f) *flea*
pulpo (m) *octopus*
pulsera (f) *bracelet*
punta (f) *tip (end)*
puro (m) *cigar*

Q

que *than*
¿qué? *what?*
quemadura (f) *burn*
quemadura de sol (f) *sunburn*
quemar *to burn*
querer *to want, love*
querido *dear (person)*
queso (m) *cheese*
¿qué tal? *how are you?*
¿quién? *who?*
quince *fifteen*
quirófano (m) *operating room*
quisquillas (f pl) *shrimp*
quizás *maybe, perhaps*

R

rábano (m) *radish*
radiador (m) *radiator*
radio (f) *radio*
rápido *fast, quick*
raro *rare (uncommon)*
rastrillo (m) *rake*
rata (f) *rat*
ratón (m) *mouse*

raya (f) *part (hair)*
rebajas (f pl) *sale (at reduced prices)*
rebeca (f) *cardigan sweater*
recado (m) *message*
recepción (f) *reception*
recepcionista (m/f) *receptionist*
receta (f) *prescription*
recibo (m) *receipt*
recobrar algo *to get something back*
recogida (f) *pickup (postal)*
récord (m) *record (sports, etc.)*
recuerdo (m) *souvenir*
redondo *round (circular)*
regalo (m) *gift;* **el regalo de cumpleaños** *birthday present*
regla (f) *ruler (for measuring)*
reír *to laugh*
rejilla de equipajes (f) *luggage rack*
relajarse *to relax*
religión (f) *religion*
relleno (m) *filling (in sandwich, cake)*
reloj (m) *clock, watch*
remar *to row*
remolque (m) *trailer*
remos (m pl) *oars*
resaca (f) *hangover*
reserva (f) *reservation*
reservar *to book*
resfriado (m) *cold (illness);* **tengo un resfriado** *I have a cold*
respirar *to breathe*
restaurante (m) *restaurant*
resto (m) *rest, remainder*
retrasado *delayed;* **el autobús se ha retrasado** *the bus is late*
reunión (f) *meeting*
revelar *to develop (film)*
revista (f) *magazine*
rico *rich*
rímel (m) *mascara*
rincón (m) *corner (of room)*
riñón (m) *kidney*
río (m) *river*
rizos (m pl) *curls*
robar *steal;* **lo han robado** *it's been stolen*
robo (m) *robbery*
roca (f) *rock (stone)*
rock (m) *rock (music)*
rodilla (f) *knee*
rojo *red*
ron (m) *rum*

ropa (f) *clothes;* **la ropa de cama** (f) *bed linen;* **la ropa interior** *underwear;* **la ropa sucia** *laundry (dirty)*
rosa (adj) *pink*
rosa (f) *rose*
roto *broken*
rotonda (f) *roundabout*
rotulador (m) *felt-tip pen*
roulotte (f) *camper trailer*
rubí (m) *ruby (stone)*
rubio *blond(e)* (adj)
rueda (f) *wheel;* **la rueda pinchada** *flat tire*
rugby (m) *rugby*
ruidoso *noisy*
ruinas (f pl) *ruins*
rulos (m pl) *curlers*

S

sábado *Saturday*
sábana (f) *sheet (bedding)*
saber *to know (fact);* **no sé** *I don't know*
sabor (m) *flavor*
sacacorchos (m) *corkscrew*
sacapuntas (m) *pencil sharpener*
sacar *to bring out*
saco de dormir (m) *sleeping bag*
sal (f) *salt*
sala de espera (f) *waiting room*
sala de pediatría (f) *children's ward*
salchicha (f) *sausage*
salida (f) *exit, departure;* **las salidas** *departures;* **la salida de emergencia** *emergency exit*
salmón (m) *salmon*
salón (m) *lounge (in hotel)*
salsa (f) *sauce*
¡salud! *cheers! (toast)*
sandalias (f pl) *sandals*
sangre (f) *blood*
sartén (f) *frying pan*
sauna (f) *sauna*
secador (de pelo) (m) *hairdryer*
seco *dry*
sed *thirsty;* **tengo sed** *I'm thirsty*
seda (f) *silk*
segundo (m) *second (noun; adj);* **de segunda** *second class*
seguro (m) *insurance;* (adj) *sure, safe (not dangerous)*

seis *six*
sello (m) *stamp*
selva *rainforest*
semáforo (m) *traffic lights*
semana (f) *week;* **la semana pasada** *last week;* **la semana que viene** *next week*
seminario (m) *seminar*
semi-seco *medium-dry (wine)*
señal (f) *deposit*
sencillo *simple*
senderismo (m) *hiking*
señor *Mr., sir*
señora *Mrs., madam*
señorita *Miss*
separado *separated*
septiembre *September*
ser *to be*
serio *serious*
seropositivo *HIV positive*
servicio (m) *service, department;* **el servicio de habitaciones** *room service;* **el servicio de radiología** *X-ray department;* **el servicio de urgencias** *emergency department*
servicios (m pl) *restrooms;* **los servicios de** *caballeros men's room;* **los servicios de señoras** *ladies' room*
servilleta (f) *napkin*
sesenta *sixty*
setas (f pl) *mushrooms*
setenta *seventy*
seto (m) *hedge*
si *if, whether*
sí *yes*
Sida (m) *AIDS*
siempre *always*
siete *seven*
significar: ¿qué significa esto? *what does this mean?*
siguiente *next*
silla (f) *chair;* **la silla de ruedas** *wheelchair*
sillita de ruedas (f) *stroller*
simpático *friendly*
sin *without;* **sin plomo** *unleaded*
sinagoga (f) *synagogue*
sitio (m) *room, space;* **el sitio web** *website*
sobre (m) *envelope*
sobre todo *especially*
sobrina (f) *niece*
sobrino (m) *nephew*
soda (f) *soda water*
sofa (m) *sofa*
sofocante *stuffy*

sol (m) *sun*
solo *alone;* **yo solo** *by myself*
sólo *just, only*
soltero/soltera (m/f) *single (unmarried)*
solución limpiadora (f) *soaking solution (for contact lenses)*
sombrero (m) *hat*
sombrilla (f) *sunshade*
somnífero (m) *sleeping pill*
somos *we are*
son *they are*
sonreír *to smile*
sonrisa (f) *smile*
sopa (f) *soup*
sordo *deaf*
sostén (m) *bra*
sótano (m) *basement*
soy *I am;* **soy de ...** *I come from ...*
spray (m) *inhaler (for asthma, etc.);* **el spray antipulgas** *flea spray*
su (s) *its/hers/his/your (formal);* **¿es suyo esto?** *is this yours?*
subirse *to get in, get on (of train, bus, etc.)*
sucio *dirty*
sudadera (f) *sweatshirt*
Sudamérica *South America*
sudar *to sweat*
sudor (m) *sweat*
suelo (m) *floor;* **el suelo aislante** *groundsheet*
sueño (m) *sleep*
suerte (f) *luck;* **¡suerte!** *good luck!*
supermercado (m) *supermarket*
suplemento (m) *supplement*
supositorio (m) *suppository*
sur (m) *south*

T

tabaco (m) *tobacco*
tabla de windsurfing (f) *sailboard*
tableta de chocolate (f) *bar of chocolate*
tacón (m) *heel (shoe)*
taller (m) *garage (for repairs)*
talón (m) *heel (foot)*
talonario de cheques (m) *checkbook*
también *too (also)*
tampones (m pl) *tampons*
tan *so;* **tan bueno** *so good*

tanto: no tanto *not so much;* **tanto ... como ...** *both ... and ...*
tapiz (m) *tapestry*
tapón (m) *cap* (bottle), *plug* (sink)
taquilla (f) *box office, ticket office*
tarde (f) *evening;* (adj) *late; it's getting late* **se está haciendo tarde**
tarifa (f) *fare*
tarjeta (f) *card;* **la tarjeta de banco** *bank card;* **la tarjeta de crédito** *credit card;* **la tarjeta de embarque** *boarding pass;* **la tarjeta de vista** *business card;* **la tarjeta telefónica** *phonecard*
tarta (f) *cake* (large)
taxi (m) *taxi*
taza (f) *cup*
té (m) *tea*
techo (m) *ceiling*
teclado (m) *keyboard*
técnico (m) *technician*
tejado (m) *roof*
tejanos (m pl) *jeans*
tela (f) *material* (cloth)
teleférico (m) *cable car*
teléfono (m) *telephone;* **el teléfono móvil** *cell phone*
televisión (f) *television;* **la televisión por cable** *cable TV*
temperatura (f) *temperature*
temprano *early*
tenedor (m) *fork*
tener *to have;* **tengo** *I have;* **no tengo** *I don't have;* **¿tiene?** *do you have?;* **tengo que irme** *I have to go;* **tengo calor** *I feel hot;* **tengo que ...** *I must ...*
teñir *to bleach* (hair)
tenis (m) *tennis*
tenue *faint* (unclear)
tercero *third*
terminal (f) *terminal*
ternera (f) *veal*
terraza (f) *terrace*
testigo (m) *witness*
tía (f) *aunt*
tiempo (m) *time, weather*
tienda (f) *store, shop;* **la tienda de comestibles** *grocery store;* **la tienda de discos** *record store*

tienda (f) *tent*
¿tiene ...? *do you have ...?*
tierra (f) *land, soil*
tijeras (f pl) *scissors*
timbre (m) *bell* (door)
tinta (f) *ink*
tinto *red* (wine)
tintorería (f) *dry cleaner*
tío (m) *uncle*
tirantes (m pl) *suspenders*
tirar de *to pull*
tirita (f) *adhesive bandage*
toalla (f) *towel*
toallitas para bebé (f pl) *baby wipes*
tobillo (m) *ankle*
toca: me toca a mí *it's my turn*
tocadiscos (m) *record player*
tocar *to feel* (touch)
todavía *yet;* **todavía no** *not yet*
todo *everything, all;* **eso es todo** *that's all*
todos *everyone*
todos los días *every day*
tomar *to take;* **tomar el sol** *to sunbathe*
tomate (m) *tomato*
tónica (f) *tonic*
torero (m) *bullfighter*
tormenta (f) *storm*
tornillo (m) *screw*
toro (m) *bull*
torre (f) *tower*
tortilla (f) *omelet*
tos (f) *cough*
toser *to cough*
tostada (f) *toast*
trabajar *to work* (job)
trabajo (m) *job, work*
tractor (m) *tractor*
tradición (f) *tradition*
traducir *to translate*
traductor/traductora (m/f) *translator*
traer *to fetch*
tráfico (m) *traffic*
traje (m) *suit* (clothing)
tranquilo *quiet*
trapo del polvo (m) *duster*
trasero (m) *bottom* (part of body)
tréboles (m pl) *clubs* (cards)
trece *thirteen*
treinta *thirty*
tren (m) *train*
tres *three*
triste *sad*

tú *you* (informal)
tu (s) *your* (informal); **tu libro** *your book;* **tus zapatos** *your shoes;* **¿es tuyo esto?** *is this yours?*
tubería (f) *pipe* (for water)
tubo de escape (m) *exhaust*
tuerca (f) *nut* (for bolt)
tuerza (a la izquierda/derecha) *turn* (left/right)
túnel (m) *tunnel*
turismo (m) *sightseeing*
turista (m/f) *tourist*

U

último *last* (final)
ultramarinos (m) *grocer*
un/una *a*
uña (f) *finger nail*
único *single* (only)
universidad (f) *university*
uno *one*
urgente *urgent*
usar *to use*
uso (m) *use*
usted *you* (formal)
utensilios de cocina (m pl) *cooking utensils*
útil *useful*
uvas (f pl) *grapes*

V

vacaciones (f pl) *vacation*
vacío *empty*
vacuna (f) *vaccination*
vagón (m) *car* (train); **el vagón-restaurante** *restaurant car*
vainilla (f) *vanilla*
vale *OK*
valle (m) *valley*
válvula (f) *valve*
vapor (m) *steam, steamer* (boat); **al vapor** *steamed*
vaqueros (m pl) *jeans*
varios *several*
vaso (m) *glass* (for drinking)
váter (m) *toilet*
¡váyase! *go away!*
veces: a veces *sometimes*
vegetariano *vegetarian*
vehículo (m) *vehicle*
veinte *twenty*
vela (f) *sailing; candle*
velocidad (f) *speed*

venda (f) *bandage*
vender *to sell*
veneno (m) *poison*
venir *to vome;*
 ¡venga aquí!
 come here!
ventana (f) *window*
ventas (f pl) *sales*
ventilador (m) *fan*
 (ventilator)
ventisca (f) *blizzard*
ver *to see;* **no veo**
 I can't see
verdad *true;* **es verdad**
 it's true; **¿verdad?** *isn't*
 that so?
verde *green*
verdulería (f)
 greengrocer
verdura (f) *vegetables*
verja (f) *gate*
vestido (m) *dress*
veterinario (m) *vet*
vez: de vez en cuando
 occasionally
viajar *to travel;* **viajar**
 en avión *fly (of person)*
viaje (m) *journey;*
 el viaje de novios
 honeymoon
vida (f) *life*

vídeo (m) *video (film);* **el**
 (aparato de) **vídeo**
 video recorder
videocámara (f)
 camcorder
vídeo juegos (m pl)
 computer/video games
viejo *old*
viento (m) *wind*
viernes *Friday*
vigilante nocturno (m)
 night porter
vinagre (m) *vinegar*
vinatero (m)
 wine merchant
vino (m) *wine*
violín (m) *violin*
visita (f) *visit;* **las horas de**
 visita visiting hours;
 la visita con guía
 guided tour
visitante (m/f) *visitor*
visitar *to visit*
visor de imagen (m)
 viewfinder
vista (f) *view*
vitaminas (f pl)
 vitamin pills
vivero (m)
 garden center
vodka (m) *vodka*

volar *to fly (plane, insect)*
volver *to come/get back,*
 return; **nos volvemos**
 mañana *we get back*
 tomorrow
voz (f) *voice*
vuelo (m) *flight*

W, Y, Z

web site (f) *website*
whisky (m) *whiskey*
y *and*
ya *already*
yo *I*
yogur (m) *yogurt*
zanahoria (f) *carrot*
zapatería (f) *shoe store*
zapatilla (f) *washing machine*
zapatillas (f pl) *slippers*
zapatos (m pl) *shoes;* **los**
zapatos de deporte
 athletic shoes
zona peatonal (f)
 pedestrian zone
zoo (m) *zoo*
zumo *juice* (m); **el zumo de**
 frutas *fruit juice;* **el zumo**
 de naranja *orange juice;*
 el zumo de tomate
 tomato juice

Acknowledgments

The publisher would like to thank the following for their help: Isa Palacios and Maria Serna for the organization of location photography in Spain; Restaurant Raymon at Mi Pueblo, Madrid; Magnet Showroom, Enfield, London; MyHotel, London; Peppermint Green Hairdressers, London; Coolhurst Tennis Club, London; Kathy Gammon; Juliette Meeus and Harry.

Language content for Dorling Kindersley by **g-and-w publishing**
Managed by **Jane Wightwick**
Editing and additional input: **Cathy Gaulter-Carter, Teresa Cervera, Leila Gaafar**

Additional design assistance: **Phil Gamble, Lee Riches, Fehmi Cömert, Sally Geeve**
Additional editorial assistance: **Kajal Mistry, Paul Docherty, Lynn Bresler**
Picture research: **Louise Thomas**

Picture credits

Key: *t=top; b=bottom; l=left; r=right; c=centre; A=above; B=below*

p2 **DK Images**: Joan Farre; p4/5 **Alamy**: Image Source tl; **Alamy**:D Hurst bl; Indiapicture bcl; p10/11 **Alamy**: BananaStock cAr; **Getty**: Taxi / James Day cBl; **Ingram Image Library**: bl; p12/13 **Alamy**: Dynamics Graphics Group / Creatas cBr; John Foxx cAr; RubberBall br; **DK Images**: cl; **Ingram Image Library**: tl, cAr, cBr, bcr; p14/15 **DK Images**: tcr; **Dreamstime.com**: Slobodan Mračina (cl); **Ingram Image Library**: cl, cBl, cAr, cBr, bcr; p16/17 **Getty**: Taxi / James Day bcr; **Ingram Image LiBrary**: tr; p18/19 **DK Images**: David Murray tr; p22/23 **DK Images**: cl, Andy Crawford cAr; Susanna Price br; Magnus Rew tcrB; **Ingram Image Library**: tcr; p24/25 **DK Images**: clA, Dave King tcr; p26/27 **Alamy**: Dynamic Graphics Group / Creatas cl; p28/29 **DK Images**: John Bulmer tcr; Dave King cr; Matthew Ward bclA; **Ingram Image Library**: bcrA, bcl cr; p30/31 **Alamy**: Comstock Images bcl Think Stock bclA; **DK Images**: cl; p34/35 **Dreamstime.com**: Slobodan Mračina (cb); **Ingram Image Library**: tcr; **iStockphoto.com**: nicolas_ (tl); p36/37 **DK Images**: bcl, bcr; Magnus Rew cl; **Dreamstime.com**: Slobodan Mračina (cla); **Ingram Image Library**: bl; **iStockphoto.com**: nicolas_ (cla/sim card); p38/39 **Alamy**: Imageshop / Zefa Visual Media cl; **Ingram Image Library**: cr; p40/41 **DK Images**: Peter Wilson bl; **Lee Riches**: cl; p42/43 **Alamy**: Image Source tcr, cAr, cAAr; p44/45 **Alamy**: Jon Arnold Images br; ImageState / Ethel Davies bl; Vikki Martin cbl; Peter Titmuss bcrr; **Alamy**: Iain Davidson Photographic bcll; David O'Shea bcr; Courtesy of Renault: c; p46/47 **Alamy**: Imageshop / Zefa Visual Media br; **Ingram Image Library**: cr; Courtesy of Renault: tcrB; **Lee Riches**: bcl; p48/49 **Alamy**: Balearic Pictures c; **Alamy**: Brand X Pictures bcl; **DK Images**: tcr, bcl; Neil Lukas bcr; John Miller crA; **Lee Riches**: cl; p50/51 **Alamy**: Peter Titmuss cr; **Lee Riches**: c; p52/53 **Alamy**: Jean Dominique Dallet tcr; **Alamy**: Image Farm Inc cAr; Imageshop - Zefa Visual Media tcrB; **DK Images**: cl; p54/55 **Alamy**: Jackson Smith cBl; **Alamy**: Brand X Pictures cl; John Foxx c; Image Source cAr; ThinkStock tcr; **DK Images**: Andy Crawford bcl; p56/57 **Alamy**: Balearic Pictures clA; **Alamy**: Brand X Pictures clAA; **DK Images**: cl; Neil Lukas tl; John Miller tcll; **Lee Riches**: tcl; Courtesy of Renault: bc; p58/59 **Alamy**: Michael Juno tcr; **Alamy**: Brand X Pictures cBl, cBBl; Ingram Publishing cAAl; **DK Images**: cAl; Max Alexander cBr; p60/61 **123RF.com**: shutswis (cb); **Alamy**: Robert Harding Picture Library bcr; **Alamy**: Image Source cAr; **DK Images**: Steve Gorton bl, tcrB; Pia Tryde cAAr; **Ingram Image Library**: cr; p62/63 **DK Images**: Stephen Whitehorn c; p64/65 **Alamy**: Arcaid bcrA; Mike Kipling c; **Alamy**: GKPhotography cBr; Goodshoot cAAr; Justin Kase tcrB; **DK Images**: Steve Tanner cAr; **Ingram Image Library**: tcr; p66/67 **Alamy**: Arcaid tl; **Alamy**: Ingram Publishing cAr; **DK Images**: tr; Stephen Whitehorn bl; **Ingram Image Library**: br; p68/69 **Alamy**: Balearic Pictures cr; directphoto.org cAr; Doug Houghton cl; Indiapicture clB; **Alamy**: CoverSpot cBl; **Lee Riches**: cBr; p72/73 **Alamy**: imagebroker tcrB; Image Source cAr; Comstock Images tcr; **Avery Weight-Tronix**: bl; p74/75 **Alamy RF**: Doug Norman bl; **Ingram Image Library**: c; p76/77 **Alamy**: Balearic Pictures bl; Indiapicture bl; **Alamy**: Coverspot clB; p78/79 **Alamy**: Luca DiCecco bcl; Steve Hamblin bcr; p80/81 **Getty**: Taxi / Rob Melnychuk bc; **Ingram Image Library**: cAr; Xerox UK Ltd: tcr; p82/83 **Alamy**: wildphotos.com tcr; **Alamy**: FogStock cAAl; Momentum Creative Group cAl; Shoosh / Up the Res cBl; **Ingram Image Library**: cl; p84/85 **Alamy**: Brand X Pictures cr; fl **Alamy RF**: BananaStock bl; Comstock Images c; SuperStock tr; **Ingram Image Library**: crB; p86/87 **Alamy**: Luca DiCecco bcl; **Getty**: Taxi / Rob Melnychuk tc; p90/91 **Alamy**: Brand X Pictures tcr; **DK Images**: cl; David Jordan cAr; Stephen Oliver cr; **Ingram Image Library**: cBr; p82/93 **Alamy**: Pixland cr; **DK Images**: cl; Guy Ryecart tr; p94/95 **Alamy**: David Kamm cl; Phototake Inc bcl; **Alamy**: Comstock Images cr; ImageState Royalty Free bcr; **DK Images**: Stephen Oliver tcr; p96/97 **Alamy**: Pixland br; **DK Images**: tl; **Ingram Image Library**: tr; p98/99 **Alamy**: Andrew Linscott c; Shotfile cr; **Alamy**: Bildagentur Franz Waldhaeusl bl; ThinkStock br; **Dreamstime.com**: Alexandre Dvihally (tl); p100/101 **DK Images**: Steve Gorton tcr; p102/103 **Alamy**: Hortus b; D Hurst tcrB; **Alamy**: image100 tcr; Barry Mason cAAr; **Ingram Image Library**: cAr; p104/105 **DK Images**: Paul Bricknell cl(6); Jane Burton bcl; Geoff Dann cl(2); Max Gibbs cl(4); Frank Greenaway cl(3); Dave King cl(1), cAr; Tracy Morgan c(5); p106/107 **Alamy**: Shotfile cr; **Alamy**: Barry Mason br; p110/111 **Alamy**: Think Stock cr; **DK Images**: Andy Crawford cr; p112/113 **Alamy RF**: Dynamic Graphics Group / Creatas tcr; image100 bl; **Ingram Image Library**: cl; bcrA; p114/115 **Alamy**: John Cole cr; **Alamy**: Image Source cAr; Index Stock cAl; jackhollingsworth.com tcr; p116/117 **Alamy**: Dynamics Graphics Group / Creatas clA; John Foxx clB; p118/119 **Alamy**: D Hurst c; **Alamy**: Pixland cr; p120/121 **Alamy**: ImageState / Pictor International cl; Shotfile cBl; **Alamy**: Sarkis Images tcr; **DK Images**: bcl; p122/123 **Alamy**: BananaStock cA; **Ingram Image Library**: cl; p124/125 **Alamy**: ImageState / Pictor International bclA; Shotfile cBl; **DK Images**: bcl; Paul Bricknell tc(5); Geoff Dann tc(3); Max Gibbs tc(1); Frank Greenaway tc(2); Dave King tc(4); Tracy Morgan tc(6); **Ingram Image Library**: bl; p126/127 **Alamy**: Jean Dominique Dallet clB; **Alamy**: Imageshop - Zefa Visual Media blA; Image Farm Inc bl; p128 **DK Images**.

All other images **Mike Good**.